AROUND paris WITH KIDS

by Emily Emerson

Fodor's Travel Publications
New York • Toronto • London • Sydney • Auckland

www.fodors.com

D0054795

CREDITS
Writer: Emily Emerson

Series Editor: Karen Cure
Editor: Andrea Lehman
Editorial Production: Tom Holton
Production/Manufacturing: Yexenia M. Markland

Design: Fabrizio La Rocca, *creative director*;
Tigist Getachew, *art director*
Illustration and Series Design: Rico Lins, Keren Ora
Admoni/Rico Lins Studio

ABOUT THE WRITER
Emily Emerson is an American writer who moved to France
for a year in 1979 and can't seem to leave. These days she
and her 9-year-old daughter divide their time between
Paris and their ramshackle 15th-century farmhouse in the
Loire Valley.

ISBN 0–679–00725–3
ISSN 1533–5313
First Edition

Important Tip
Although all prices, opening times, and other details in this
book are based on information supplied to us at press time,
changes occur all the time in the travel world, and Fodor's
cannot accept responsibility for facts that become outdated
or for inadvertent errors or omissions. So always confirm
information when it matters, especially if you're making a
detour to visit a specific place.

Special Sales
Fodor's Travel Publications are available at special discounts
for bulk purchases for sales promotions or premiums. Special
editions, including personalized covers, excerpts of existing
guides, and corporate imprints, can be created in large
quantities for special needs. For more information, contact
your local bookseller or Special Markets, Fodor's Travel
Publications, 280 Park Avenue, New York, NY 10017.
Inquiries from Canada should be directed to your local
Canadian bookseller or sent to Random House of Canada,
Ltd., Marketing Dept., 2775 Matheson Boulevard East,
Mississauga, Ontario L4W 4P7. Inquiries from the United
Kingdom should be sent to Fodor's Travel Publications, 20
Vauxhall Bridge Road, London, England SW1V 2SA.

PRINTED IN THE UNITED STATES OF AMERICA
10 9 8 7 6 5 4 3 2 1

COUNTDOWN TO GOOD TIMES

GET READY, GET SET!

Everyone knows that organizing a family's schedule is a full-time job, whether you're juggling activities at home or planning the perfect vacation. Spending time together shouldn't be another chore to figure out, especially when you're supposed to be relaxing and enjoying yourselves.

We know what it's like to try to find good places to take your children or grandchildren, especially when you're in a strange city with a limited amount of time and energy. Sometimes it's tough to find out when places are open, whether they're likely to be crowded or even sold out, and what age group they're geared to. There's nothing like bringing a "grown-up" 12-year-old to an activity that's intended for his 6-year-old sister. And if you're planning a trip to Paris, it's harder still to figure out the best things to do before you even get there. That's where we come in.

What you'll find in this book are 68 ways to have a terrific couple of hours or an entire day with children in tow. Paris is crammed with things for kids to do, even if you don't speak French. We've scoured the city, digging out activities your kids—and you—will love, from the state-of-the-art kids' museum in the La Villette complex to a traditional puppet theater in the Jardin du Luxembourg. Open the book to any page and find a helpful description of a kid-friendly attraction, with age ratings to make sure it's right for your family, smart tips on visiting so that you can get the most out of your time there, and family-friendly eats nearby. The address, telephone number, open hours, and admission prices are all there, too. We've done the work, so you don't have to.

To find out about special events, contact the Office de Tourisme de la Ville de Paris (127 av. Champs-Élysées, tel. 01–49–52–53–54) or the Espace du Tourisme d'Ile de France (Carrousel du Louvre underground shopping mall, 99 rue de Rivoli, tel. 01–44–50–19–98). Check out the free English-language publications *Paris Free Voice* and *FUSAC* (France-USA Contacts), available at W.H. Smith bookstore (248 rue de Rivoli) and other locations. For information in French on weekly events, try *Pariscope* and *Frimousse*, available at newsstands. *Paris-Mômes*, an excellent, free bimonthly supplement covering events just for kids, appears in *Libération* newspaper and is distributed in various shops and museums.

WAYS TO SAVE MONEY

We list only regular adult and kids' prices; children under the ages specified are free. It always pays to ask at the ticket booth whether any discounts are offered for a particular status or affiliation (but don't forget to bring your I.D.). Many attractions offer family tickets or long-term memberships. Keep an eye out for attractions—mostly museums and other cultural destinations—that offer free admission one day a month (usually Sunday) or one day a week after a certain time.

The Carte Musées et Monuments (available at tourist offices and métro stations) gets you into 70 local museums at a discount and without standing in line; one-day or three-day cards are available. Special transportation-plus-admission tickets are offered for many attractions just outside Paris; we've indicated many in this book. The Carte Orange, with unlimited métro and bus travel for a month, can be a big money-saver; choose your card by the number of zones you expect to visit. A two-zone card covers central Paris and the near suburbs, and kids' cards are available at a discount. The Paris-Visite card, sold at all métro and train stations, furnishes unlimited travel on area métros, trains, and buses for one to five days; passes for kids 4–11 are half price. This card also grants discounts to a number of attractions.

DINING OUT

Paris restaurants are generally more expensive than their U.S. counterparts, but most offer kids' menus or will prepare a special kids' meal on request. Yes, you can find kids' hamburgers and steaks (specify *bien cuit* if you don't want them served rare) and *frîtes* (french fries), but realize that French-style fast food is more likely to consist of crêpes, *croque-monsieur* sandwiches (grilled ham and cheese), and baguette sandwiches. Other on-the-go options can be picked up at *charcuteries* (takeout meat and food shops) and *pâtisseries* (pastry shops). If you're planning on a picnic, however, be warned that most city parks don't let you sit, or even walk, on the grass (though it's generally fine to do so in the city's *bois*, or woods). No matter. Do what the French do, and have your picnic on a park bench.

GETTING AROUND

Paris is divided into 20 *arrondissements* (administrative districts), each with its own character and its own *mairie* (city hall). We list arrondissements in the French manner (e.g., 6e is the 6th arrondissement), following addresses.

The Paris métro system is fast, efficient, economical, and generally safe; it closes at around 1 am. One ticket per person lets you ride as far as you like within central Paris. Kids' tickets are discounted. A 10-ticket *carnet* is more economical than buying separate tickets; a Carte Orange (see above) is the best choice if you're planning a long stay. The RER system (suburban commuter trains, such as the ones that run to the two Paris airports) requires separate RER tickets, available from ticket booths in all RER stations. Keep your ticket during the ride to show conductors and to exit from the train stations.

Paris buses are fun for kids, but the system is sometimes difficult to follow. (Pick up a "Paris Bus" brochure at any métro station.) You can pay with a métro ticket or cash, but each time you change buses, you must pay again.

WHEN TO GO

With the exception of seasonal attractions, kid-oriented destinations are generally busiest when children are out of school—especially weekends, Wednesdays (when many French schools either organize field trips or have no classes), holidays (especially two-week school vacations in mid-February, at Easter, and in mid-November), and July and August. Most sights are less crowded at meal times (1–2 and 7–9).

The hours we list are the basic hours, not necessarily those applicable on holidays. Some attractions are closed when schools are closed, but others add extra hours on these days. It's always best to check if you want to see an attraction on a holiday.

SAFETY

Obviously the amount of vigilance necessary will depend on the attraction and the ages of your kids. Traffic is heavy throughout Paris, and sidewalks are small and crowded. Be especially careful crossing streets; many drivers run red lights. Skaters and even scooter-riders often take short-cuts on sidewalks. On the métro, watch for the gap between platforms and cars, and hold children's hands when boarding. Avoid empty métro cars late at night.

When you arrive at an attraction, point out to your kids what the staff or security people are wearing, and find a very visible landmark to use as a meeting place, should you get separated. Most staff people at Paris tourist attractions speak some English. If you do split into groups, pick a time and place to meet.

FINAL THOUGHTS

Actually, this time it's yours, not ours. We'd love to hear what you or your kids thought about the attractions you visited. Or if you happened upon a place that you think warrants inclusion, by all means, send it along, so the next family can enjoy Paris even more. You can e-mail us at editors@fodors.com (specify the name of the book on the subject line), or write to us at Fodor's Around Paris with Kids, 280 Park Avenue, 10th floor, New York, NY 10017. We'll put your ideas to good use. In the meantime, bon voyage!

THE EDITORS!

AQUABOULEVARD

Paris may be in northern Europe, but you'd never know it once you step into this water-lovers' wonderland. A year-round indoor-outdoor water park, Aquaboulevard lets you take a trip to the tropics without leaving the heart of the city. In summer, Aquaboulevard's outdoor beach and pool area, open June–August, is one of the city's most popular sunbathing spots.

Feel like basking on the sand? You can, on the artificial beach surrounding the outdoor pool. Want to bodysurf? The waves won't please experienced surfers, but small kids enjoy jumping them. Tired of sidewalks, buildings, and traffic noise? The landscape here surrounds you with tropical vegetation and the sounds of flowing water. You can also swim through fountains, get splashed by waterfalls, wade in a river, and—most popular among kids—careen through tunnels and down long slides that end with a splash into a pool. (Different

KID-FRIENDLY EATS Aquaboulevard is within the Forest Hills commercial complex, which also contains a branch of family-friendly **Hippopotamus** (tel. 01–53–98–91–20) and fast-food outlets. At cozy **Le Numide** (75 rue Vasco-de-Gama, tel. 01–45–32–13–13), you can sample couscous, *bourek* (flaky pastry with cheese inside), and other North African treats. For more on the water theme as well as a splurge, visit the **River Café** (146 quai de Stalingrad, Issy-les-Moulineaux, tel. 01–40–93–50–20), in a nearby suburb. This barge on the Seine is a trendy but friendly restaurant. See also Parc André Citroën.

4–6 rue Louis-Armand, 15e.
Métro: PL.-Balard

01–40–60–10–00

 78 frs. ages 13 and up,
58 frs. children 3–12;
admission is for 4 hrs

 M–Th and Sa 9 AM–11 PM,
F and Su 9 AM–12 AM

2 and up

age groups have different slides.) Parents aching from too much sightseeing can relax in bubbling hot tubs, and though kids might not need the tubs' therapeutic benefits, they do like the bubbles.

A star attraction here is the life-size model of a whale commissioned by Jacques Cousteau, the late French explorer and film personality who did so much to increase awareness of aquatic environments throughout the world. Because all 27 meters (90 feet) of Madame Whale is hollow, kids can crawl inside and get a close-up look at a whale's inner workings. A gentle slide leading out into a pool is the preferred exit, even for the smallest kids. Children who favor dry land have a special play area where they don't even have to get wet. All in all, the complex is one of the city's best antidotes to stress.

KEEP IN MIND
Because Aquaboulevard is central Paris's only water park, it can get extremely crowded, especially on hot summer days. To avoid the crush in July and August, try to come during meal times (noon–2 or 7–9).

HEY, KIDS! When you hear a loud toot, it means surf's up—the wave machine is about to turn on. If you happen to be in one of the pools when this happens (after 2:30 only), get ready to ride the waves. When you climb the ladders to the top of the tall water slides, look for the lights, and don't set off until you see the green one. The system was designed so you won't end up sliding down on top of someone else (and so no one will come sliding down on you).

ARC DE TRIOMPHE

One of the world's best-known memorials to military might, this massive monument dates from the early 19th century, but its first years were as up-and-down as the fortunes of the man who had it built.

The Arc de Triomphe (Arch of Triumph) was commissioned by Napoléon in 1806 to commemorate his victory at the Battle of Austerlitz. Little more than the foundations had been finished by 1810, when Napoléon married, so a wood-and-canvas mock arch was erected for the celebrations. When Napoléon lost at Waterloo in 1815, the monument was put on hold. It was finally finished in 1836, in time for Napoléon's coffin to be hauled through it in a grandiose funeral procession in 1840. Today, the arch is the site of France's tomb of the unknown soldier, where a flame has been kept burning since 1923; it's rekindled every evening at 6:30.

KEEP IN MIND To check out the carvings on the outside of the arch (representing—what else?—war scenes), you'll need to be on the sidewalks on the outer edges of the place Charles-de-Gaulle. The carving entitled *Le départ des volontaires* (Departure of the Volunteers) is considered the best.

KID-FRIENDLY EATS **Alléosse** (13 rue Poncelet, tel. 01–46–22–50–45) is a reliable cheese store on a lively food-market street. **Maison Pou** (16 av. Ternes, tel. 01–43–80–19–24) has served delicious charcuterie since 1830, before the arch was finished. **Lina's Sandwiches** (8 rue Marbeuf, tel. 01–47–23–92–33) has American-style sandwiches, quiches, and salads for here or to go. **Del Papa** (233 bis rue du Faubourg-St-Honoré, tel. 01–47– 63–30–98) has tasty pizza, and **La Maison du Chocolat** (225 rue du Faubourg-St-Honoré, tel. 01–42–27–39–44) is chocolate heaven. See also Palais de la Découverte and École Lenôtre.

Pl. Charles-de-Gaulle, 8e. Métro:
Charles-de-Gaulle–Étoile

 40 frs. adults 26 and up,
25 frs. ages 12–25

 Apr–Sept, daily 9:30 AM–11 PM;
Oct–Mar, daily 10 AM–10:30 PM

 01-55-37-73-77

 8 and up

As far as kids are concerned, though, the most interesting thing about the Arc de Triomphe isn't its history but the view from the top, 45 meters (150 feet) above the place Charles-de-Gaulle (formerly the place de l'Étoile and still called that by Parisians). You can take an elevator, but most children prefer to climb the stairs, all 300 or so of them. Halfway up is a little museum showing a film on the monument's history. From the rooftop terrace you can check out the 12 streets that radiate out from the square, including the avenue Foch, Paris's widest street. You'll see that Paris is bisected by a broad paved line leading straight from the Arc du Carrousel, in front of the Louvre, through the Arc de Triomphe all the way to the Grande Arche in the western suburb of La Défense, with the Champs-Élysées to the east of the arch and the avenue de la Grande Armée to the west. You'll also get a great view of Paris's chaotic traffic swirling nonstop through the square below you.

HEY, KIDS! From the top of the arch, Paris traffic looks totally insane, right? But there is a method to its madness. It's called *priorité à droite*, which means "whoever is on your right has the right-of-way." If you were driving into the place Charles-de-Gaulle, this is how it would work: You'd charge ahead, keeping an eye out for vehicles on your right and doing your best not to hit them. You'd never once look to your left, because whoever was there would be looking at you and staying out of your way. At least that's what you'd be hoping.

ARÈNES DE LUTÈCE

Take a trip back in time to the days before Paris was Paris—to the 1st through 3rd centuries AD, when Paris was a bustling Gallo-Roman stronghold called Lutetia, population 6,000. Hidden away behind apartment buildings in the Left Bank district, just off bustling rue Monge, is a city park with a remnant of that time: the Arènes de Lutèce (Lutetia Arena).

Built into a hillside, the arena was used for circus and theatrical productions until around AD 280, when invading barbarians destroyed it and most other Gallo-Roman structures on the Left Bank. For 1,600 years the arena was forgotten, and then at the end of the 19th century its ruins were unearthed when a line of the Paris métro was constructed nearby. The arena's first use after rediscovery, however, was as a parking lot for buses.

Today the Arènes de Lutèce has been excavated and refurbished, but only to the extent that its stonework is now solid and secure. The city wisely chose not to make the ancient

KID-FRIENDLY EATS Pick up some goodies and picnic with Parisians on the arena's stone steps. An open-air market on the place Monge operates Wednesday, Friday, and Sunday mornings, while the nearby rue Mouffetard has an even wider selection of food shops, open Tuesday to Sunday. Other good bets are **La Ferme des Arènes** (60 rue Monge, tel. 01–43–36–37–38), a delicious cheese store; **La Crêpe Carré** (42 rue Monge, tel. 01–43–26–99–98), for classic main-dish and dessert crêpes; and **Le Jardin des Pâtes** (4 rue Lacépède, tel. 01–43–31–50–71), serving organic vegetarian dishes.

Rue des Arènes, 5e. Métro:
Pl. Monge

 Free

08–36–68–31–12
Office de Tourisme

Daily 8–sunset

All ages

structure into a museum, but rather to give it new life as a public park. The plan worked. The arena is one Paris monument that doesn't feel like a monument at all. Locals love to come here; tourists rarely seek the place out. Just as thousands of aristocratic Lutetians used to enjoy themselves watching performances, today's parents enjoy sitting on the stone seats watching their kids play soccer in the arena's sandy ring. Children who don't like soccer love to climb around on the steep stone benches.

The north side of the arena has a cool, shady little park with a gurgling fountain, a play area for smaller kids with a sandbox and jungle gyms, and several benches. That combined with the rest of the arena makes it a perfect spot for a picnic.

KEEP IN MIND
Steep stone stairs and walls without guardrails are dangerous for children under 5, particularly toddlers. Smaller children can safely play on the level court in the center of the arena, however, or in the park and play area on the arena's north side.

HEY, KIDS! Want to know how Paris got its name? A tribe of Gauls called the Parisii lived on what's now the Ile de la Cité (the island in the Seine that's home to Notre-Dame) from the 3rd century BC to the arrival of the Romans in 52 BC. The Romans beat the Gauls and built their own city—named Lutetia—which contained the arena, some public baths, a long aqueduct, and other structures. After the barbarians destroyed Lutetia in AD 280, a group of Gauls rebuilt the city and, in 360, named it Paris, in honor of their ancestors.

AU NAIN BLEU

65

Seen one toy store and you've seen 'em all, right? Well, not quite. Au Nain Bleu (At the Blue Dwarf) is Paris's oldest toy store, founded in 1836. That alone isn't reason enough to come here, of course, but Au Nain Bleu has a lot more than venerability going for it. It carries one of the biggest selections of toys in Paris, including toys you won't see anywhere else—mainly because there just aren't that many people who can afford them. Even if you're not in the mood to bring home the store's huge 10,000-franc stuffed donkey, however, you can still enjoy seeing all those playthings, many of them actually affordable.

The store is crammed floor-to-ceiling with toys of all kinds. Kids love getting a close look at hundreds of stuffed animals, checking out the electric trains humming around, and examining the elaborately furnished doll houses. In fact, you'll find a huge array of dolls and doll-related items here, including furniture, clothes, and wigs. There's also an extensive collection of board games, including the Parisian version of Monopoly.

HEY, KIDS! What do the kids in your school play at recess? In Parisian elementary schools, recent fads have included marbles, Pokémon cards, and jump rope (girls only). One thing that never goes out of style is soccer, played by girls *and* boys.

KEEP IN MIND Other excellent Paris toy stores are Si Tu Veux (68 Galerie Vivienne, 2e, tel. 01–42–60–59– 97); Au Bon Marché (22 rue de Sèvres, 7e, tel. 01–44– 39–80–00), a department store; and Nature et Découvertes (see below). La Fabrique des Jouets en Bois (3 rue des Prouvaires, 1er, tel. 01–40–41–07–21), Centre Kapla (27 rue de Montreuil, 11e, tel. 01–43–56–13–38), and Atelier de la Bonne-Graine (16 pass. de la Bonne-Graine, 11e, tel. 01–43–47–40–47) give toy-making classes for kids (in French).

Merchandise spans children of all ages, from babies to active older kids. If your child can dream of a toy, it's probably here; if it's not, the store will order it for you.

Au Nain Bleu puts on special toy-related exhibits from time to time, including boundless stuffed bunnies and baskets at Easter and spectacular window displays at Christmas. Though parents appreciate the store's early 19th-century architecture, kids are usually more interested in running around the store and touching and playing with the toys that Au Nain Bleu leaves out for just that purpose. The ground-floor display of giant stuffed animals—giraffes, elephants, panthers, the donkey, and more—is sure to thrill younger kids, even though they aren't supposed to touch these horrendously expensive creatures. Au Nain Bleu's staff isn't always friendly, but your kids probably won't even notice that. Besides, it isn't often you come upon a monument to kid-pleasing that's endured for 165 years.

KID-FRIENDLY EATS Both **Fauchon** (26–30 pl. de la Madeleine, tel. 01–47–42–60–11) and **Hédiard** (21 pl. de la Madeleine, tel. 01–43–12–88–88) are chic restaurants serving gourmet takeout. Fauchon also has a tearoom. For a bargain lunch in this very high-priced neighborhood, duck into **La Tonkinoise** (7 rue de Castellane, tel. 01–42–66–62–96), which has good *nems* (Vietnamese-style egg rolls) and other Vietnamese treats. See also Champs-Élysées, Palais de la Découverte, Opéra Garnier, Musée Grévin, and Jardins du Palais-Royal.

BATEAUX PARISIENS

Kids can't help but love *bateaux mouches,* the tourist boats that chug up and down the Seine through central Paris. With their big glass roofs and huge spotlights illuminating Paris monuments at night, they look impossibly garish. Once on board, however, you'll be rewarded with a spectacularly beautiful view of the city as seen from the water, a reminder that Paris has been a river port for thousands of years. (As for the term *bateaux mouches,* which actually means "fly boats," it comes from the Les Mouches district of Lyon, where the boats were originally manufactured.) Of all the tour boat operators—and there are many—a sound choice is Bateaux Parisiens, which is particularly good for the younger set.

Regular cruises begin near the Eiffel Tower and set off for a one-hour voyage that takes you up the river under various bridges, including the Passerelle des Arts (the footbridge leading between the Louvre and the Left Bank), to Notre-Dame on the Ile de la Cité. The boat turns around the island and then heads back downstream past the Louvre and the

KEEP IN MIND If you'd like to cruise the Seine but aren't interested in loud-speaker commentary, try the Batobus (tel. 01–44–11–33–44), a leisurely water taxi that makes seven stops. You can get off at any stop, paying according to how far you travel, or take the entire voyage (65 frs. ages 12 and over, 35 frs. children 11 and under). To find the stops, look for the little Batobus signs along the quais of the Seine. Boats operate April–May and October, daily 10–7, and June–September, daily 10–9.

Port de la Bourdonnais, 7e. Métro: Bir-Hakeim-Grenelle

 01–44–11–33–44
www.bateauxparisiens.com

50 frs. ages 12 and over, 25 frs. children 11 and under; Croisière Enchantée 45 frs.

 Apr–Oct, daily 10 AM–11 PM every ½ hr; Nov–Mar, daily 10–9 every hr; Croisière Enchantée Oct–Mar, Sa–Su 4

All ages; kids' cruises 10 and under

Eiffel Tower to tiny Ile des Cygnes (Island of the Swans), which it circles before returning to the dock. Don't miss the replica of sculptor Frédéric-Auguste Bartholdi's Statue of Liberty on the end of the Ile des Cygnes. (The real statue was built in Paris in 1886.) Throughout the cruise, a loudspeaker tells you about what you're seeing—in French, English, Spanish, and finally German. The only catch is that only the French narration is synched with the sites. By the time you're told in English that you're passing under the Passerelle des Arts, for example, you've already passed it.

On weekends, a special Croisière Enchantée (Enchanted Cruise) is geared to kids under 10 and their parents. A pair of elves (professional actors) entertain you by singing songs and telling stories (in French) about the monuments you're sailing past. Now where else can you find singing elves on the Seine?

KID-FRIENDLY EATS On a hot summer day, treat yourself to ice cream at **Bac à Glaces** (109 rue du Bac, tel. 01–45–48–87–65). Every possible flavor of ice cream and sherbet is on hand, all scooped into homemade cookie-type cones. See also Tour Eiffel.

HEY, KIDS! Paris is divided into Left Bank (Rive Gauche) and Right Bank (Rive Droite), referring to the banks of the Seine from the point of view of a person sailing downstream (with the current). If your boat is traveling upstream toward Notre-Dame and the narration points out the Musée d'Orsay on the Left Bank, you should actually look to your right. The Louvre, on the Right Bank, will be on your left. Got it? Watch people turn their heads back and forth trying to figure out what's going on.

BOIS DE BOULOGNE

The vast Bois de Boulogne (Boulogne Woods) was once a wild, dangerous forest where the kings of France hunted wolf, deer, and wild boar. (It's still unwise to venture into its wooded areas at night.) Napoléon III gave the forest to Paris in the mid-19th century, and developer Baron Haussmann, who was carving huge boulevards through the city at the time, laid boulevards through the woods as well, modeling his plan on London's Hyde Park. Today, the park is popular among Parisians looking for fresh air and open spaces.

There are two lakes here: the Lac Inférieur (the larger one), where you can rent paddleboats, and the Lac Supérieur, where kids bring remote-controlled boats and buzz them around the lake. The park contains two race courses, too: the Hippodrome d'Auteuil (tel. 01–70–71–47–47), which stages steeplechases (with jumps and hurdles) regularly March–December, and the Hippodrome de Longchamp (tel. 01–44–30–75–00), which hosts flat racing April–October. On the first Sunday in October, you can watch top Thoroughbreds compete in the world's richest horse race, the Arc de Triomphe.

KEEP IN MIND Although many of the Bois de Boulogne's attractions are near métro stops, you'll need a car or bicycle to tour the whole park. Bikes can be rented near the entrance to the Jardin d'Acclimatation (see below) and near the boat ramp at the Lac Inférieur.

KID-FRIENDLY EATS Within the park are three worthwhile restaurants. The **Relais du Bois de Boulogne** (carrefour Croix-Catalan, tel. 01–42–15–00–11), in a gorgeous setting, has a popular fixed-price buffet, a children's play area, and a petting zoo. **L'Auberge du Bonheur** (allée de Longchamp, tel. 01–42–24–10–17) has a beautiful outdoor terrace and reasonable prices. Reservations aren't taken, so arrive by 12:30 for lunch and 7:30 at dinner. Take a little boat to **Le Châlet des Iles** (tel. 01–42–88–04–69), a magical—and expensive— restaurant on the island in the Lac Inférieur.

Main entrances: Porte Maillot, Porte de la Muette, Porte de Passy, 16e. Métro: Porte d'Auteuil, Porte Dauphine, Porte de la Muette, Porte de Passy

Daily 24 hrs

08–36–68–31–12 Office de Tourisme

Free

All ages

There is a bird sanctuary near the Grande Cascade (an artificial waterfall), and the gorgeous Parc de Bagatelle contains a little château built in 1755 by the Count d'Artois, Marie Antoinette's brother-in-law; it's now used for temporary art exhibits. But this area's main draw is its fabulous flowers, especially May's irises and June's roses. While parents enjoy the blooms, kids can run off steam or have a close encounter with the resident birds—shy ducks and proud peacocks, who roam around spreading their tails and screeching.

The Pré Catalan, in the park's center, includes the Jardin de Shakespeare, with plants mentioned in the bard's plays. In summer, open-air Shakespeare productions (some in English) are held near here. The bois's grassy open areas attract Paris-based U.S. expats, who come to play baseball and football, and French people who play soccer and rugby. And there's plenty of room for just running around.

HEY, KIDS! Steeplechase racing has been held at the Hippodrome d'Auteuil since 1870. Why do they call it steeplechasing? Centuries ago in England, horses and riders would race from one village's church steeple to another, jumping over hedgerows and fences all along the way. Today's obstacles are built to look like the ones from those old courses: fence-like hurdles, tall jumps covered with tree branches, and even wide ditches. If you go to a race at Auteuil, follow the crowds (with your parents!) to the middle of the course to get a close-up view of the huge horses pounding past you.

BOIS DE VINCENNES

Just east of Paris's city limits, the 500-acre-plus Bois de Vincennes (Vincennes Park) is the city's biggest park and well worth a métro ride. Contained within its borders are a number of terrific attractions for kids and families, both indoors and out.

In the former category, the imposing Château de Vincennes, built in the 1300s in the middle of what was once a royal hunting preserve, is worth a visit for its sumptuous gilded interiors. You'll find more gilt on a huge statue of Buddha—the largest in Europe—in a Buddhist temple overlooking the Lac Daumesnil.

Most of the Bois de Vincennes's best attractions, however, are outdoors. There's the Parc Zoologique de Paris and the Parc Floral de Paris (see separate listings for both) as well as three lakes: the Lac de Saint Mandé, the Lac Minimes, and the Lac Daumesnil, around which you can watch a puppet show, take a turn on a merry-go-round, eat *barbe à papa* (cotton candy), rent a paddleboat, or just sit on a bench and watch the world go by. The park is

HEY, KIDS! Try imagining some of what's happened in the Bois de Vincennes in its long history. The word Vincennes comes from Vilcena, the name of a huge primeval forest (with wild animals and bandits) that existed here in Gallo-Roman times. In the 9th century, monks began holding a fair here, and a fair is still held every year (Easter through May), though it's now called the Foire du Trône and is mainly a huge amusement park with roller coasters. In the 13th century, France's great king St. Louis judged criminals under an enormous, ancient oak tree in the Vincennes woods.

Main entrance: av. Daumesnil, 12e.
Métro: Porte Dorée

 Park free, some
attractions charge

 Daily 24 hrs; attraction hrs vary

08-36-68-31-12 Office de Tourisme,
01-43-28-47-63 Ferme de Paris

 All ages

crisscrossed with bike lanes, jogging paths, and sidewalks popular with rollerbladers and skateboarders. You'll find plenty of places to picnic as well as huge expanses of grass for running, walking, and even rolling; a number of soccer fields; bike-rental outfits (near the Château de Vincennes and the Lac Daumesnil), and such other sports facilities as the Hippodrome de Vincennes (a horse-racing track).

One of the most kid-oriented attractions is the Ferme de Paris (rte. de Pésage, near the Hippodrome), a real working farm run by a young couple. Children can sometimes help feed the animals (pigs, chickens, goats, lambs, and more), and there's an orchard, a vegetable garden, and fields of wheat and sunflowers, which are harvested by tractor.

KEEP IN MIND
Though patrolled, the park can attract unsavory types. Avoid coming here at night, and be careful where you picnic; sometimes the lawns are not clean. It's best to keep to areas within sight of other people, especially groups.

KID-FRIENDLY EATS There are many snack bars and small cafés clustered around the Lac Daumesnil and the Lac des Minimes, including **Le Chalet des Îles** (on an island in the Lac des Minimes, tel. 01-43-07-77-07), which has a lovely outdoor terrace. The Bois de Vincennes also makes a great picnic destination; in city "parks" access to grass is usually strictly controlled, but in these "woods" you can spread out as much as you like and actually sit on the lawn. Pick up treats at a charcuterie (take-out meat and food shop) or pâtisserie (pastry shop), and choose a spot.

CATACOMBES

You don't have to have ghoulish tendencies to enjoy a visit to Paris's underground graveyard, but it helps. Walk down 90 steps to a huge complex of subterranean caverns stacked floor to ceiling with skeletons—around 6 million of them. Most have been artfully arranged, with row upon row of skulls set upon crossed tibias. The overall effect is like being on the set of a horror movie, reinforced by the title "The Empire of the Dead" indicated on the catacomb's brochures. Guides try to play down the macabre aspects, but with all those skeletons, what can they do?

The catacombs were originally quarries, yielding rocks used in the great buildings, roads, and aqueducts of the pre-Paris, Gallo-Roman stronghold of Lutetia. The quarries had been largely forgotten when, in 1785, someone had the idea to solve Paris's cemetery overcrowding problem by placing skeletons in the underground caves. Several million skeletons from the La Cimetière des Innocents (Cemetery of the Innocents) and others were then hauled here.

KEEP IN MIND You should judge whether your kids are likely to be intrigued or scared by all the bones. Guides light your way as you tour the shadowy caverns, but it's a good idea to bring your own pocket flashlight, as well as a jacket.

HEY, KIDS! The French resistance fighters who made the catacombs their Paris headquarters during World War II were a highly organized group of spies within their own country. In 1940, Germany occupied Paris, controlling the city until France's allies, American and British troops, liberated it in 1944. During the German occupation, some Parisians chose to collaborate with the Germans, while others fled or organized undercover resistance to German rule. Working in small groups whose members usually did not know each others' real names, members of the Résistance spied on the Germans, sheltered escaped prisoners, and staged sneak attacks.

1 pl. Denfert-Rochereau, 14e. Métro: Denfert-Rochereau

 40 frs. adults, 22 frs. children 8–18

 T–F 2–4, Sa–Su 9–11 and 2–4

01–43–22–47–63

7 and up

A guide leads you through chilly, cramped corridors—each marked with the name of the street above it—and past stacks of bones. It's as though you're seeing Paris from a ghost's point of view. Indirect lighting, which casts shadows of bones onto the sides of the tunnels, reinforces this Halloween atmosphere. Perhaps the most impressive aspect of the catacombs is their size, especially when you realize that you are taken through only a small part of this vast subterranean world, totaling 65 kilometers (40 miles) of tunnels.

A small catacombs museum comes as a relief after your walk through the world of bones. Displays on the long history of this strange Paris underworld include its use as a secret headquarters of the Résistance (French resistance fighters) during Paris's occupation by German troops during World War II. Around 50,000 visitors tour the catacombs every year and survive, proving that there are no dangers here, just the thrill of glimpsing Paris's creepy side—a far cry from the lively boulevards just a few feet above.

KID-FRIENDLY EATS Le Palais d'Or (71 rue de la Tombe-Issoire, tel. 01–43–27–66–26) sells yummy croissants, along with decadent pastries. Unfortunately, it's closed Sunday afternoon, Monday, and Tuesday. Le Zeyer (234 av. du Maine, on pl. d'Alésia, tel. 01–45–40–43–88) is a big, bustling brasserie serving delicious sole meunière (sole in butter sauce), classic steak-frites (steak with french fries), and tarte Tatin (upside-down apple tart). For a taste of home, visit McDonald's (5 av. Général-Leclerc, tel. 01–43–22–35–53). See also Médaillons d'Arago.

CATHÉDRALE DE NOTRE-DAME-DE-PARIS

Small children may be disappointed not to see the Disney version of Quasimodo, the Hunchback of Notre-Dame, scrambling around on the cathedral's rooftops, but at least they can check out the gargoyles. France's most famous cathedral was built from 1163 to around 1345 on a spot that had already been considered holy for centuries. Take time to walk all the way around the cathedral to view the spectacular rose window above the main entrance; the gargoyles; the flying buttresses, added in the 14th century to support the structure's walls so that larger windows could be installed; and the magnificent Cloister Portal on the cathedral's north side, created in around 1250. A little park behind the cathedral has swings and benches and is always crowded with mothers, toddlers, and tourists.

Although most of Notre-Dame's original stained-glass windows have been lost over time and the church's interior can get very crowded with tour groups, it's still a thrill to stand within the vast space where for centuries the kings and queens of France were crowned. The main appeal of Notre-Dame for most kids, however, is the chance to climb up to the

HEY, KIDS! Among Notre-Dame's scowling stone gargoyles is one with a trunk. Eons ago, a herd of woolly elephants, *Elephas primigenius*, apparently hung out on the heights of eastern Paris in what is now Buttes-Chaumont park. A tooth from one of these prehistoric creatures was discovered in 1903, when Line 3 of the Paris métro system was being installed. Archaeologists have determined that the trail the elephants followed down to the Seine to drink ended up just across the river from where Notre-Dame stands today, so it's appropriate that there's one stone elephant on the cathedral. Can you find him?

Pl. du Parvis-de-Notre-Dame, 4e.
Métro: Cité

 Cathedral free; tower 35
frs. adults 26 and up, 23
frs. ages 12–25

 Cathedral daily 8–6:45;
tower daily 10–5:30

01-42-34-56-10

 5 and up

cathedral's roof. The stairs—which are steep and plentiful—begin at the base of the north tower. The reward for your climb is a spectacular view of the Seine and the Ile de la Cité. Above you, in the south tower, the cathedral's great bell, known as Emmanuel, weighs 13 tons and is tolled only on momentous occasions.

In front of the church, the square known as the Parvis (from "Paradise") is the place to which all signposts throughout the country refer when they give distances to Paris. Beneath the Parvis, the aptly named *crypte archéologique* has vestiges of Gallo-Roman rooms.

To get the best view of the front of Notre-Dame, cross the Pont au Double (in front of the cathedral) and head to the Left Bank's peaceful little square Viviani. Here you can gaze at this great architectural treasure while having an impromptu park-bench picnic.

KEEP IN MIND

Paris's poignant monument to Parisians deported by the Nazis during World War II is found in the square de l'Ile de France, at the very tip of the Ile de la Cité, behind Notre-Dame. The memorial contains the tomb of the unknown deportee.

KID-FRIENDLY EATS **Hippopotamus** (9 rue Lagrange, tel. 01–43–54–13–99), a restaurant chain geared to carnivores, offers crayons, balloons, and a good fixed-price kids' menu. The **Crêperie des Arts** (27 rue St-André-des-Arts, tel. 01–43–26–15–68) has crêpes of all kinds, from main-dish *galettes* (hearty buckwheat-flour crêpes) to delicate dessert crêpes. **Mirama** (17 rue St-Jacques, tel. 01–43–29–66–56) has a wide choice of Chinese dishes, and **La Fourmi Ailée** (8 rue du Fouarre, tel. 01–43–29–40–99) is a tearoom/restaurant/library with good salads, fine pastries, and killer hot chocolate.

CENTRE DE LA MER ET DES EAUX

Let's hit the beach—or rather the ocean—right here in the heart of Paris! This oceanographic center founded in 1906 by Prince Albert I of Monaco is aimed at making people—especially kids—more sensitive to life forms in marine and other aquatic environments. The center has six aquariums (from 500 to 4,000 liters) that show different types of sea creatures in their natural habitats, from the cold waters of the Atlantic to a tropical coral reef. All are filled with vividly colored animal and plant life sure to please children.

Some of the museum's exhibits are accessible even to very small children. In the "Qui mange qui?" ("Who eats whom?") display, kids line up blocks to see which organisms are at the top and bottom of the food chain. In the "A qui sont ces beaux yeux?" ("Whose pretty eyes are these?") exhibit, youngsters try to match up photos of creatures' eyes with photos of the whole creatures. When you get it right, a bell rings.

KEEP IN MIND Although most of the center's documentation is in French, the fish and turtles themselves require no translation. In addition, many exhibits are very tactile, so even non-French-speaking kids should thoroughly enjoy their visit.

KID-FRIENDLY EATS Polidor (41 rue Monsieur-le-Prince, tel. 01–43–26–95–34) is a Paris institution, known to generations of tourists and locals as a good bet for inexpensive family-style French cooking served at big, family-size tables. You may get routed into the back room, where foreigners are often seated, but never mind; just dig in. **Le Jardin des Pâtes** (4 rue Lacépede, tel. 01–43–31–50–71) has organic, vegetarian dishes that include full-flavored soups, pasta with vegetables, and eggy, fruit-filled *clafouti* (a puffy pancake) for dessert. See also Jardin des Plantes, Jardin du Luxembourg, and Muséum National d'Histoire Naturelle.

A big amphitheater is home to film screenings (in French) of the Jacques Cousteau team conducting experiments all over the world and educational puppet shows during France's two-week-long February and November school vacations. The center also puts on special temporary exhibits throughout the year.

One of the most thought-provoking exhibits here is the turtle orphanage: a terrarium filled with turtles of various sizes. The center makes a policy of taking in turtles that were bought as pets and then abandoned when they became too big or too aggressive. In so doing, it hopes to educate children about the responsibilities of asking for and caring for a pet, just as it hopes to educate all visitors about their impact on marine life.

HEY, KIDS! As far as clown fish go, it takes all kinds. They all prefer to live in very close quarters with hospitable sea anemones, though. Among *Amphiprion percula* clown fish, one fish in the school (call him a bully) always grows a lot bigger than the others. He hogs the biggest anemone, while his schoolmates may go homeless. *Amphiprion perideraion*, on the other hand, is a family-oriented clown fish, with mom, dad, and the kids sharing an anemone. *Chormis viridis* is a single parent—a dad who gets an anemone ready and raises his kids there alone.

CENTRE NATIONAL D'ART ET DE CULTURE GEORGES POMPIDOU

The Centre Pompidou (Pompidou Center in English, but referred to by Parisians as "Beaubourg," after its neighborhood) was a big city-planning gamble. Former president Georges Pompidou and crew picked a vacant lot in the middle of Paris as the site for a "supermarket for culture" and proceeded to create an edifice that looks like a kid might have built it using Legos and Tinkertoys. Today the recently renovated center is popular among all sorts of Parisians, including children, who come for all sorts of reasons.

Thanks to its wacky architecture, the center is a hit with kids as soon as they see it. From the exterior, you see brightly painted ducts and supports, clearly showing why Parisians nicknamed this place "Notre-Dame des Tuyeaux" ("Our Lady of the Pipes"). Kids also love the big square in front, which is always filled with fire-eaters, sword-swallowers, mimes, and musicians. It's an ongoing, free outdoor circus.

Visitors flock inside to do research in the public library, see films in the movie theaters

KEEP IN MIND For kids, guided tours called "Apprendre à Regarder" ("Learn to Look") and arts workshops called "Les Ateliers des Enfants" (based on the current children's gallery exhibit) are held Wednesdays, Saturdays, and school holidays. Kids can take one workshop or a three-workshop series. A recent choice was "Entrez dans la Danse, Voyez Comme l'Art Danse" ("Join the Dance, See How Art Dances"), combining dance and art appreciation. Guided tours for families are offered monthly on a Sunday (25 frs. children over 3). These programs are in French. For information and reservations, visit the ground-floor "Espace Éducatif" desk or call 01–44–78–49–13.

Rue Beaubourg, 4e. Métro: Hotel-de-Ville, Rambuteau

01–44–78–12–33,
01–44–78–44–22 Cinema 2
www.centrepompidou.fr

Center free; art museum 30 frs. adults 18 and up, 50 frs. with temporary exhibits; kids' films 20 frs.

Center W–M 11–10, art museum W–M 11–9; kids' gallery W–M 11–6

3 and up;
kids' gallery 6–12

or live performances in the new Grande Salle (Large Hall), or view the stunning collection in the Musée National d'Art Moderne (National Museum of Modern Art). Even small children enjoy the art here, especially the Alexander Calder mobiles, the weird mechanical structures of Jean Tinguely, Pablo Picasso's *Petite fille sautant à la corde* (*Little Girl Jumping Rope*), and the vibrantly colored and shaped paintings of Matisse, Léger, and Soutine.

In La Galerie des Enfants, a gallery space geared to kids, you'll find special interactive art exhibits (two per year). A recent show focused on musical comedy, with stunning costumes kids could touch and music kids could listen to through headphones. Every Wednesday at 2, the center's Cinema 2 shows films for kids 7 and up (in French, reservations required). And if it's kid-pleasing vistas you're after, take an elevator that runs through a glass tube up the west side of the building. The view is spectacular, especially at sunset.

HEY, KIDS! Check out the crazy fountain in square Igor Stravinsky, next to the center. It was created in honor of the famous musician by two artists with very different styles: Jean Tinguely (robots) and Niki de Saint-Phalle (colorful pieces, including big red lips that will probably squirt you).

KID-FRIENDLY EATS The center's top-floor **café,** reached by the glass-walled elevator, has great views and lots of low-priced choices. Spacious, popular **Café Beaubourg** (100 rue St-Martin, tel. 01–48–87–63–96) has sandwiches, light meals, pastries, and drinks, and it's open almost all the time. **Dame Tartine** (2 rue Brisemiche, tel. 01–42–77–32–22) serves quiches, salads, and other affordable treats. You can sit outside next to the wacky fountain in square Igor Stravinsky and let the kids run around. See also Jardin des Halles, Musée Picasso, and Place des Vosges and the Marais.

CHAMPS-ÉLYSÉES

57

If there's one Paris street that people have heard of, it's the avenue des Champs-Élysées—Les Champs to Parisians. This wide street, whose name (translation: "Elysian Fields") suggests paradise, is a paradise for shoppers, window-shoppers, and strollers eager to be part of the action.

Once known as the most beautiful avenue in the world and a popular setting for 19th-century Parisian family outings, the boulevard evolved into a bustling high-rent commercial district whose sidewalks became parking lots. (As proof, note that the Champs-Élysées is the French Monopoly equivalent of Park Place.) Over the past few years, efforts have been made to restore some of the avenue's former beauty by planting trees and reclaiming the sidewalks for pedestrians. Families have returned, and the sidewalks are once again wide enough to walk, push a stroller, and even toddle without getting jostled by other pedestrians—not the case on most Paris streets. Shopping options appeal to all ages:

HEY, KIDS!
Not surprisingly, Paris's oldest Guignol puppet theater has its oldest Guignol puppet, and he's worth more than a lot of the avenue's fancy jewelry. (Guignol is the character with the long black ponytail.) You can recognize him by his green and red jacket; other Guignols wear brown jackets.

KEEP IN MIND Keep a close eye on children as you walk the avenue. Car traffic on the cross streets can be heavy and fast, as can skaters, cyclists, and skateboarders. Keep an eye on the clock and calendar, too. Guignol puppet shows (17 frs.) are performed Wednesday, Saturday, Sunday, and holidays at 3, 4, and 5. The stamp and pin market is held Thursday, Saturday, Sunday, and holidays. Note that the big movie theaters on the Champs-Élysées often show films in English with French subtitles. If a U.S. film is billed as "v.o." (*version originale*), it's being shown in English.

from an enormous Virgin Megastore (#52) for preteens and teens to a Disney Store (#44) for character-loving youngsters. On foot, you'll realize something you probably wouldn't notice from a car: The Champs-Élysées has a fairly steep slope from the place de la Concorde up to the Arc de Triomphe. Keep this in mind if you've got toddlers or a stroller along, and start your journey from the Arc.

At the place de la Concorde end, you'll find the Jardins des Champs-Élysées. Here you can take the kids to Les Marionnettes du Rond-Point des Champs-Élysées, Paris's oldest Guignol puppet theater (founded 1818), or check out the lively stamp and pin market. But beware: Though stamp collectors might love examining the wares, prices are high. You can also take a peek through heavily guarded gates at the Palais d'Élysée (France's White House) and at the nearby U.S. Embassy, on the avenue Gabriel.

KID-FRIENDLY EATS Your kids are bound to like **Dragons Élysées** (11 rue de Berri, tel. 01–42–89–85–10), where they can eat above an aquarium, with big fish swimming underfoot. Reserve a table *sur le sol en verre* ("on the glass floor"). The fixed-price lunch is the best deal; it's not cheap, but it's copious enough for two kids to share. **Aux Pains Perdus** (39 rue de Berri, tel. 01–43–69–09–29) is a reliable sandwich shop, though its high stools aren't convenient for small kids. See also the Arc de Triomphe, Jardin des Tuileries, and Palais de la Découverte.

CHÂTEAU DE VERSAILLES

To kids, the Château de Versailles and its over-the-top gilded luxury may seem more like a theme park than the palace of French kings. While most children aren't overly impressed by its rich furnishings and sumptuously decorated rooms, they do find much to interest them, both in the château and especially out.

Even kids can't resist the gorgeous Galerie des Glaces (Hall of Mirrors); the Salon d'Apollo (Throne Room), dripping with gold; and the Chambre du Roi (King's Bedroom), big enough for an army. Watch for images of the sun, in honor of Louis XIV (the Sun King). Louis was jealous of another chateau, Vaux-le-Vicomte, which belonged to his own finance minister. So he had Versailles built, using the same architect (Le Vau), to prove who was boss.

Outside the château, a vast formal park—created by the architect Le Nôtre (designer of Vaux-le-Vicomte's gardens and Paris's Tuileries)—is filled with statues, fountains, and elegant perspectives. It's a great place to run off steam, but don't imagine you can explore it all

KEEP IN MIND Individual audio guides, available in English and for rent at the château's main entrance, help you keep the château's history and contents straight. Kids like wearing the earphones. Guided tours of both the château and park are available in English, but if you understand French, consider the excellent tours for kids and families (tel. 01–30–83–77–80). Don't miss Les Grandes Eaux Musicales, when the park's fountains are turned on and set to music (May–September, Sunday at 11, 3, and 5:20), and the Grande Fête de la Nuit sound-and-light extravaganzas held in summer.

Town of Versailles

 Château 45 frs.
ages 26 and up, 35 frs.
ages 18–25, after 3:30
free; park free

Château June–Sept, T–Su 9–6;
Oct–May, Tu–Su 10–5; park daily
sunrise–sunset

01-30-84-74-00,
01-40-67-10-04 mock farm
www.chateauversailles.fr

 3 and up

on foot; it's much too big for that. Tour it by bicycle (rentals at the porte St-Antoine entrance and near the Grand Canal) or on a little mock train that starts from the château's north terrace. Paddling a four-person boat around the Grand Canal is also fun (March–October, rental stand at La Petite Venise).

The Petit Trianon is an elegant little château in the park, built by Louis XV for his mistress, Madame de Pompadour, and later given by ill-fated King Louis XVI to Marie-Antoinette. Ask a guide to show you the ingenious disappearing mirrors, which slid out of the floor to cover the windows at night. Young kids like the Hameau de la Reine (queen's hamlet), a mock farm created by Marie-Antoinette so she could play at being a farm woman (albeit surrounded by servants). Today there's a petting zoo here; kids 5–12 who'd like to play at being Marie-Antoinette can sign up for an afternoon (Wednesday–Saturday) of brushing a donkey and feeding chickens.

TRANSPORTA-TION: Versailles is 20 kilometers (12 miles) southwest of Paris. Take the RER commuter train, line C, to the Versailles–Rive Gauche stop; there are around 60 trains a day Monday–Saturday, and 35 on Sunday. By car (30 minutes), take the A13 highway west to the Versailles-Château exit.

KID-FRIENDLY EATS **La Flotille** (tel. 01–39–51–41–58), next to the Grand Canal, has a restaurant section (lunch only), with a good fixed-price menu for parents and a tasty kids' menu, as well as a cheaper brasserie section (open all day) with lots of choices. In summer you can eat on the outdoor terrace overlooking the canal. There are also several snacks stands in the park. **Sister's Café** (15 rue des Réservoirs, tel. 01–30–21–21–22) is a relaxed, friendly restaurant where you can sample U.S. treats like chicken wings, quesadillas, and a hearty brunch in the domain of the Sun King.

CITÉ DE LA MUSIQUE

Ever had a yen to play in a gamelan (an Indonesian orchestra)? At the new Cité de la Musique (music center) complex, the whole family can take a gamelan class as well as attend a concert featuring some of the world's best musicians, check out Beethoven's very own clavichord, and see about 4,500 rare musical instruments from around the globe. Also home to France's prestigious Conservatoire Nationale de Musique (National Music Conservatory), the Cité de la Musique is another jewel in Paris's ambitious La Villette development project crown. It's a must for music-lovers.

The center's Musée de la Musique (music museum) contains the conservatory's huge collection of musical instruments as well as scale models of opera houses and concert halls with all their backstage equipment. Everything in this museum is designed with kids in mind. Among interactive displays, the most popular are headphones equipped with an infrared device, which sense when you're standing in front of an instrument and reproduce its sounds. Often kids don't want to take the headphones off when their

HEY, KIDS!

What's the difference between a harpsichord and a piano? They both have strings, but the strings of a harpsichord are plucked when keys are played, while in a piano, the strings are hit with little hammers. See if you can hear the difference through your headphones.

KID-FRIENDLY EATS **Café de la Musique** (213 av. Jean-Jaurès, tel. 01–48–03–15–91) is a big, relaxed, friendly, and trendy brasserie serving classic French cuisine (lots of grilled meat), homemade fries, inventive salads, and a good Sunday brunch. The huge terrace is popular on sunny days. **Le Bistrot du Cochon d'Or** (192 av. Jean-Jaurès, tel. 01–42–45–46–46), the more reasonably priced bistro branch of a famous local restaurant, is a carnivore's delight, harking back to the days when La Villette was Paris's slaughterhouse district. See also Cité des Sciences et de l'Industrie and Parc de la Villette.

221 av. Jean-Jaurès, 19e. Métro:
Porte-de-Pantin

01-44-84-46-00,

01-44-84-44-84 concerts and classes
www.cite-musique.fr

Museum 40 frs. adults,
15 frs. children 6–18;
concerts and classes vary

T–Th 12–6, F–Sa 12–7:30, Su 10–6

7 and up

visit is over. Special guided visits (in French) bring the world of music to life through games and stories. There's even a class for older kids (8 and up) that teaches them how to build musical instruments. Spectacles Jeune Publique (theater-music-dance performances for young audiences) are organized almost every week. After the show, kids usually get to sit and chat with the performers.

As for those gamelan classes, they're for anyone 7 or over who'd like to learn to play one of the 20 or so gamelan instruments. Never played an instrument before and can't read a note of music? Don't worry; take off your shoes, sit on the floor, and let the friendly teachers (most of whom speak English) explain the gongs, xylophones, drums, and other Indonesian instruments on hand. After a while, you'll hear yourself and your family actually making music together. Music is the universal language after all, and the center is a great place to learn how to speak it.

KEEP IN MIND Atelier de Gamelan en Famille (family gamelan workshop) classes are held in French on Sundays, October–June (50 frs. per adult, 40 frs. per child). Classes in other instruments are also offered. Spectacles Jeune Publique are usually offered on Wednesdays at 3 and Thursdays at 9:30 and 2:30 (40 frs.). Classes and special guided tours of the museum for kids 4 and up are offered on Wednesdays, Saturdays, and Sundays. Concerts featuring top musicians are given regularly in the 1,000-seat concert hall.

CITÉ DES ENFANTS

54

This children's museum within Paris's futuristic Cité des Sciences et de l'Industrie complex (see below) is without a doubt one of Paris's top stops for kids. Divided into three sections—one for ages 3–5, one for ages 5–12, and one for special exhibitions—the Cité des Enfants takes very seriously the idea that kids should have fun while they learn. Hands-on exhibits are so colorful and exciting that kids tend to run around the whole time, poking and pushing and pulling. Although children must be accompanied by an adult, no more than two adults per family are allowed in at one time, so if you're over 18, you are definitely going to be in the minority here.

Exhibits for younger kids are simple to use as well as instructive, tactile, and fun. A huge hand-operated grain grinder illustrates how wheat becomes flour. A dance floor activates a video camera, so kids can see themselves hop around. At a construction site complete

KEEP IN MIND The children's museum is open for four 90-minute visits each day (Tuesday, Thursday, and Friday 9:30, 11:30, 1:30, and 3:30; Wednesday, Saturday, and Sunday 10:30, 12:30, 2:30, and 4:30). Only a limited number of people are allowed inside at each session, so it's a good idea to come here first when you arrive at the Cité des Sciences et de l'Industrie and get tickets for the next available session. Try to avoid Saturday and Wednesday afternoons, when many day-care centers and schools bring groups here and the staff seems to let in more kids than usual.

Cité des Sciences et de l'Industrie, 30 av. Corentin-Cariou, 19e. Métro: Corentin-Cariou

01-40-05-12-12

 25 frs.

 T and Th–F 9:30–3:30, W and Sa–Su 10:30–4:30

3 and up

with hard hats, little kids can build huge structures with foam bricks, but the real hit is a whole section that lets kids get as wet as they like while diverting flowing water through channels (plastic lab coats provided).

Older kids can practice presenting a television show, do scientific experiments with sound and light, play around with state-of-the-art imaging equipment, and more. Instructors, some of whom speak English, offer optional 30-minute classes on special subjects, and, through Techno-Cité, 90-minute sessions (Wednesday and Saturday afternoons, ages 11–15) in which kids can learn how to build a robot, program a video game, or operate a helicopter flight simulator. How much more fun can learning get?

KID-FRIENDLY EATS In addition to the food outlets within the museum complex, you'll find shops on the avenue Corentin-Cariou where you can buy picnic goodies to eat in the Parc de la Villette (see below, also Cité de la Musique and Cité des Sciences et de l'Industrie).

HEY, KIDS! The museum's aquarium is home to fish native to the Mediterranean, a sea off France's southern edge that covers 1,145,000 square miles and was once filled with countless varieties of aquatic life. Today, however, 100 million people live on the Mediterranean coastline, and 85% of the sewage from coastal cities is piped directly into the sea. Plus, the Mediterranean is constantly crossed by oil tankers and other huge ships spewing out their own pollutants. Luckily a number of countries, including France, are now working hard to clean up this beautiful body of water before it's too late.

CITÉ DES SCIENCES ET DE L'INDUSTRIE

I t's hard to believe when you first spot the high-tech exterior of this huge museum complex that the site was once home to a ramshackle slaughterhouse in one of Paris's grubbiest neighborhoods. The Cité des Sciences et de l'Industrie (Museum of Science and Industry), a product of inspired city planning, shows that Paris has its foot firmly planted in the 21st century. Everything about this place is cutting-edge, from its architecture to its user-friendly exhibits.

The museum's huge, 9,500-square-meter (102,000-square-foot) Explora section has almost 20 departments full of interactive gadgets that most of us never got to play with in science class. They're all designed to teach schoolchildren (and adults) about a wide range of subjects, including communication, images, outer space, sounds, math, medicine, oceans, volcanoes, computer science, and the gardens of tomorrow. Top kid hits are the Jeux de Lumière (Light Games), which attract even the most blasé Nintendo player; a display on sound

KEEP IN MIND Long lines can build up at the planetarium and the Géode before each day's shows begin. Although both theaters' shows are in French, the images are so stunning that kids should enjoy themselves even if they can't understand the narration.

KID-FRIENDLY EATS The museum complex contains several places to eat, including a self-service **cafeteria** within the Cité des Sciences where everyone in your group can taste individual portions of classic French fare. **Croq Cité,** at the museum's entrance, has French-style fast food (*croque monsieur* sandwiches, fries). **La Tartine** (25 av. Corentin-Cariou, tel. 01–40–36–22–81) has a wide choice of sandwiches and some salads. **Le Relais Villette** (25 av. Corentin-Cariou, tel. 01–40–36–91–17) is an authentic 1950s bistro with good food and reasonable prices. See also Cité des Enfants and Parc de la Villette.

Parc de la Villette, 30 av.
Corentin-Cariou, 19e.
Métro: Corentin-Cariou

08-36-68-29-30
(English message available)
www.cite-sciences.fr

50 frs. adults (Su 35 frs.),
35 frs. children 7–17

M–Sa 10–6, Su 10–7

3 and up

deflectors, which lets you whisper and be heard 15 meters (50 feet) away; and the automobiles section, where you can test-drive a car using a simulator. There's even a whole museum just for 3- to 12-year-olds (see Cité des Enfants).

You could spend days just exploring Explora, but the museum complex offers much more. The gleaming silver Géode dome shows mind-boggling IMAX films on a 1,000-square-meter (over 10,000-square-foot) hemispherical screen, and the 300-seat Le Planétarium has shows on the galaxy. You can tour the Argonaute, a spy submarine built during the Cold War for the French navy, and gaze into a huge aquarium that's home to 200 species. The Louis Lumière cinema shows 3-D films (in French), and the Cinaxe takes kids on virtual trips, perhaps into outer space or to the bottom of the sea. Cool! This is one museum where your children are almost certain to play happily for hours without whining once—and they're sure to learn something, too.

HEY, KIDS! Take a hike—down the middle of the solar system. The planetarium's deep, dark space tunnel (it's better than a black hole) lights up with every step you take and gives you a *Star Wars* view of the galaxy. And thanks to the museum's radio telescopes you can actually hear the heartbeats of the stars. Don't forget to check out the Voie Lactée (Milky Way). If you thought all stars were white, take a look at the exhibit of photos made with special light-accumulating plates, which show stars in Technicolor.

LA DÉFENSE

This contemporary concrete-and-glass commercial complex west of Paris looks from afar like a mirage. Named for a local monument honoring Paris's courageous but unsuccessful defense against Prussian forces in 1871, La Défense has been called Paris's Manhattan because of its skyscrapers. It differs from the U.S. city, though, in its lack of street life—because it has few streets. Instead, you find paved pedestrian spaces as well as parks, an open-air sculpture garden, restaurants, stores, and other attractions that humanize this ultramodern development.

La Défense's top draw is the Grande Arche de La Défense, a 90-meter-tall, 90-meter-wide (300 feet by 300 feet) squared-off arch on the extension of the line that runs from the Louvre to the Arc de Triomphe. Kids love running on the paved area under the arch, watching a huge sheet of canvas, like a giant sail, flap above their heads. (The canvas cuts the wind that gusts through the arch.) What kids like best about the monument, though, are the glass elevators that shoot up an inside wall (90 meters/300 feet in 60 seconds) to a top-

KEEP IN MIND Other attractions that make La Défense worth the train ride include the Dôme IMAX theater (1 pl. du Dôme, tel. 08–36–67–06–06), with its gigantic (1,144–square-meter/12,300-square-foot), 180° domed movie screen (57 frs. ages 5 and up). Kids are impressed by the size of the images even if they don't understand the French. Under the same roof, the Musée de l'Automobile (Car Museum) contains more than 100 rare vehicles, from very early automobiles to state-of-the-art sports cars. The museum is open daily 12:30–7:30 and costs 35 frs. adults, 20 frs. kids.

Pl. de La Défense.
RER: Grande-Arche-de-La-Défense

01–49–07–27–57
www.grandearche.com

Grande Arche 40 frs.
adults 19 and up, 32 frs.
ages 18 and under

Grande Arche daily 12:30–7:30,
sculpture garden daily 24 hrs

7 and up

floor terrace, with spectacular views of the Arc de Triomphe and central Paris. In contrast to that arch, which was dedicated to military might, the Grande Arche was conceived as a monument to *fraternité* (as in the French revolutionary slogan: *liberté, égalité, fraternité*: "liberty, equality, brotherhood") and inaugurated on the 200th anniversary of the revolution, in 1989. (Today, prosaically, it houses France's transport ministry.)

La Défense's parks are filled with monumental sculptures by 20th-century artists. The big thumb by César and the giant bronze frog by Claude Torricini are bound to get kids' attention. *Le bassin* (the Basin), by Takis, includes 49 spotlights pointed toward downtown Paris. Kids can run among the artworks, and several playgrounds keep the youngest kids entertained. While the art here, all in free public spaces, shows the infinite possibilities of sculpture, La Défense itself demonstrates that contemporary business complexes don't have to be soulless.

HEY, KIDS! Gilles de Dom apparently built a "self-propelled vehicle" in Antwerp, Belgium, in 1479, but most people agree that the world's first car—a steam-powered carriage—was built in Paris by Nicolas-Joseph Cugnot in 1769. The Musée de l'Automobile's early-model cars include a motorized tricycle

KID-FRIENDLY EATS There's a **restaurant** on the top floor of the Grande Arche and, on the ground, a branch of **Hippopotamus** (2 pl. de La Défense, tel. 01–46–92–13–75), a family-restaurant chain serving good grilled meats, *frites* (fries), and kids' menus. **Marks & Spencer** (tel. 01–55–91–12–00), a department store in the Les 4 Temps shopping mall (follow signs from the Grande Arche) has tasty British-style take-out food for a park-bench picnic. **Le Bistrot de l'Arche** (38 parvis de La Défense, tel. 01–40–81–08–16) has varied cuisine, it's open nonstop 6 AM–10:30 PM and has tables outside in summer.

DISNEYLAND PARIS

Why come to Paris and visit Disneyland? Simply put, because it's there. The Magic Kingdom is an easy trip from the city and a fun break for kids. Disneyland Paris is pretty much like Disneyland in the United States, except that it's smaller and some of the names are in French. In its early days, the park was plagued by a number of problems that included—no kidding—an invasion of field mice, but now, almost a decade after it opened, Disneyland Paris is going strong. A second park may open in 2011.

There's something here for any age. Under-fours will probably be most excited by seeing their favorite Disney characters, who hang out in Town Square every morning and periodically perform at the Théâtre du Château (next to Sleeping Beauty's castle). At 3 PM daily (and again at night), the big Disney parade shows off huge floats based on classic Disney films; grab a spot on the curb of Main Street (and be prepared to defend it against late-arriving,

KID-FRIENDLY EATS The park is filled with snack bars and restaurants. **Walt's** and **Plaza Gardens** are the most expensive. Picnicking on food you've brought with you is the cheapest option, but you have to go to the designated picnic area outside the park's gates to do it.

KEEP IN MIND The quickest way (40 minutes) to cover the 32 kilometers (20 miles) from Paris east to Disneyland is by RER commuter train, line A, which stops near the park's gates. Combination Disneyland Paris–transport tickets are on sale in métro and train stations. By car, take the A4 highway toward Marne-la-Vallée; exit at Parc Disneyland. Once in the park, remember to check rides' height and age restrictions before standing in line. To avoid sensory overload, take breaks. Note that Disney hotels next to the park are convenient, fun—and expensive. Many offer two-day deals, though, and special admission offers are often available.

Marne-la-Vallée

01-60-30-60-53,
407/934-7639 from U.S.
www.disneylandparis.com

 220 frs. ages 12 and up,
170 frs. children 3-11

 Apr-Oct, daily 9-8;
Nov-Mar, M-F 10-6, Sa-Su 9-8

3 and up

pushy parents and kids). The Mad Hatter's Tea Cups ride, in Fantasyland, is a good bet for little kids, as are the Critter Corral petting zoo in Frontierland and the Videopolis shows.

Bigger kids will go for the big-thrill rides: Space Mountain, Indiana Jones and the Temple of Peril: Backwards!, and the Big Thunder Mountain roller coaster. The Star Tours ride, in Discoveryland, ends in a room filled with computer and video games that any kid suffering Nintendo withdrawal will be glad to see. The main drawbacks of Disneyland: Younger kids are bombarded with so many stimuli that they may at some point burst into tears through sheer overload, while older kids get frustrated waiting in line for an hour to enjoy a ride that's over in less than four minutes. But everyone forgets these problems when they see the fabulous fireworks display over Sleeping Beauty's castle, with Tinkerbell flitting around overhead leaving a trail of pixie dust.

HEY, KIDS! Can you find the hidden Mickeys? Here's one: In the Pirates of the Caribbean battle scene, the hole blown out of the castle wall is in the shape of a Mickey head. Here's another: When the City Hall clock's hands are 15 minutes apart, they make a Mickey head. (The hands are the ears, the center of the clock is the head.) Yet another: On the fronts of the Indiana Jones trains there's an Inca-style Mickey head. And that's just the beginning. There are hidden Mickeys throughout the park, but you have to look hard to spot them.

DOUBLE FOND

You sit down, your waiter brings you a glass of Coke, and—presto!—your glass disappears right before your very eyes! What kind of place IS this?

The Double Fond is a café-theater for people who love magic tricks. (The translation of its name refers to the double, or false, bottom on a trick box.) What sets the shows here apart from big-time magic extravaganzas in huge auditoriums is that the tricks are performed in a fairly small space right in front of you, and everyone in the audience gets a chance to participate. Kids are encouraged to get in on the act, especially at the matinees, designed especially for them. The emphasis is on card tricks and other classic sleight-of-hand numbers that have eternal appeal for youngsters. And the best part is that you and your children can enjoy a part of the city's rich and varied theater scene even if you don't speak French, since the shows are based on gestures rather than language.

KEEP IN MIND Kids' theater in French includes Aktéon Théâtre (11 rue du Générale-Blaise, 11e, tel. 01–43–68–74–62); Antre Magique (50 rue St-Georges, 9e, tel. 01–39–68–20–20); Au Café Chantant (36 rue Bichet, 10e, tel. 01–42–08–83–33), a cabaret; Comédie de Paris (42 rue Fontaine, 9e, tel. 01–42–81–00–11); Théâtre Fontaine (10 rue Fontaine, 9e, tel. 01–48–74–74–40); Théâtre des Blancs-Manteaux (15 rue des Blancs-Manteaux, 4e, tel. 01–40–30–12–15); and Théâtre Dunois (108 rue du Chavaleret, 13e, tel. 01–45–79–97–97). Théâtre du Nesle, an English-language theater, sometimes programs plays suitable for kids (8 rue Nesle, 6e, tel. 01–46–34–61–04). See also Opéra Garnier.

1 pl. du Marché-Ste-Catherine,
4e. Métro: St-Paul

 01–42–71–40–20

 60 frs. matinees,
100 frs. evenings

June–Sept, daily 8:30 PM, 10:30 PM,
and 12 AM plus Sa 3:30; Oct–May,
T–Sa 8:30, 10:30, and 12 plus Sa 3:30

Matinees 6 and up,
evenings 10 and up

You can sit at the tall stools in the downstairs bar with your eyes glued to the magician's hands just inches in front of your face, and you still won't be able to tell how the magician manages to make that ace of spades turn up where you least expect it. That is, you probably won't be able to figure it out unless you've taken one of the magic classes offered here (in French). There are special classes for kids (Saturdays 4:30–5:30, 50 frs., or 100 frs. show plus class) as well as classes for adolescents and adults. These classes are only for groups, but you can call ahead to reserve a place with a group. Everyone in the family can learn how to trick your friends back home. Invite a few people over, serve them something to drink, and—you got it!—no more glass. Tell them you learned it in Paris.

For more magic tricks, visit the nearby Musée de la Curiosité et de la Magie (see below).

KID-FRIENDLY EATS The Double Fond serves drinks but no meals. **Le Studio** (41 rue du Temple, tel. 01–42–74–10–38), for Tex-Mex, has an outdoor courtyard where kids can run around. See also Place des Vosges, Musée de la Curiosité et de la Magie, and Musée Picasso.

HEY, KIDS! Here's a simple card trick. Before you start, arrange a deck of cards with one black four on top and the other black four on the bottom. Fan the cards and ask someone to pick a card and look at it. Then, put the top half of the deck face down on a table and have the person put the selected card on top of it. Put the other half of the deck on top of the card. Then look through the deck. The card in between the two black fours will be the one the person picked.

ÉCOLE LENÔTRE POUR AMATEURS
GASTRONOMES

How would you like your kids to whip up a chocolate mousse for your next dinner party? They can learn how to do just that and a whole lot more at this cooking school for kids organized by Lenôtre, one of France's best-known names in gourmet cuisine and pastry.

The 90-minute classes are given on Wednesday afternoons all year long (in French) in a cozy kitchen meant to reproduce conditions in your own home—if your home kitchen runs to marble countertops, blue-and-white-tile walls, and a battery of saucepans in kid-pleasing bright red with white polka dots. Classes, each led by a highly trained Lenôtre chef, are limited to seven kids, so every child gets plenty of chances to ask questions and get to know fellow food-loving classmates. These are very hands-on classes that show kids how much fun cooking can be, while also teaching them basic techniques of classic French

HEY, KIDS!
In a book by the French writer Marcel Proust, a character eats a madeleine cookie and is suddenly overcome with memories of his childhood. Can you think of something to eat that would bring back memories of when you were really little?

KID-FRIENDLY EATS The on-site **Lenôtre** shop offers dozens of take-out goodies. Still hungry? **GR 5** (19 rue Gustave-Courbet, tel. 01–47–27–09–84), named for one of France's main hiking trails, features cooking from mountainous eastern France. Kids should like the stick-to-your-ribs cheese fondue or the *raclette* (melted cheese cooked at your table on a hot grill); you spread the cheese over boiled potatoes and ham. Don't forget the pickles. **Coffee Parisien** (7 rue Gustave-Courbet, tel. 01–45–53–17–17) is for when you're homesick for bagels and cream cheese, eggs Benedict, a quesadilla, or a U.S.-style burger. See also Arc de Triomphe.

48 av. Victor-Hugo, 16e. Métro: Victor-Hugo

 150 frs. per class

01-45-02-21-19

W 2–3:30 or 4–5:30

7–12

cuisine. Children won't be asked to use any dangerous kitchen equipment (recipes have been designed to avoid the need for that) but will sometimes do some chopping under the chef's watchful eye. The most-used tools are the whisk and the wooden spoon. Note that even though most of the resident chefs speak English, children need to speak at least some French to be able to follow what's going on.

Each class focuses on a particular dish. Some recent classes taught kids how to make *mousse au chocolat* (chocolate mousse), crème caramel (baked custard with caramel sauce), madeleines (in case someone wants to have a Proustian experience), *fondue au chocolat* (chocolate fondue, a very popular offering), and *bûche de Noël* (yule log, a gooey Christmas cake decorated to look like a log). The best part is that kids get to eat their creations after the class and, if there's any left over, bring some home to share with their family.

KEEP IN MIND The 150 frs. price may seem hefty, but it's a bargain compared to the price for Lenôtre's adult classes, given Monday–Tuesday and Thursday–Saturday, in French. Adult classes (six–seven people) last four hours and cost from 500 frs. (traditional breads, for example) to 1,200 frs. (a gala Christmas dinner). But you do get to eat what you prepare, not to mention being ready to wow your and your kids' friends at your next party. For any class, contact the school well in advance to find out what dishes are being taught when and to reserve a place.

LES ÉGOUTS

Come to Paris and tour the sewers? Yuck! Well, that might be your reaction, but kids seem to be enthusiastic about visiting the city's collective plumbing system. And they're not the only ones; Paris's sewer tour has become so popular that lines for it can get really long in summer. The tour's appeal seems to lie in seeing Paris's flip side: the dark, smelly underbelly of the gleaming, elegant city overhead. Don't worry; you won't have to walk in or touch anything icky.

You visit a small underground museum and an area where you pick up a brochure and see a film (in French) on Paris's public sanitation system, from its earliest days to the present. Next, you go on a tour of the sewers in action. Guides take groups through a few well-lit tunnels to show you how the system works. Each tunnel is marked with the name of the street it serves, and pipes coming from individual buildings are marked with their addresses. As in the Catacombes (see above), across town, you'll discover that there's a whole world under your feet wherever you go in Paris.

KID-FRIENDLY EATS **Thoumieux** (79 rue St-Dominique, tel. 01–47–05–49–75), a classic bistro owned by the same family for three generations, has homey French dishes at very reasonable prices. With authentic turn-of-the-last-century decor, **Poujauran** (20 rue Jean-Nicot, tel. 01–47–05–80–88) is one of Paris's best bakeries/pastry shops, famous for its sourdough baguettes, *cannelés* (soft, yeast-risen sweet cakes), and buttery *gâteau basque* (Basque pound cake). Treat yourself to sublime chocolates from **Michel Chaudun** (149 rue de l'Université, tel. 01–47–53–74–40); the peppery *ganache aux poivre* is out of this world. See also Palais de Chaillot and Tour Eiffel.

93 quai d'Orsay, 7e.
Métro: Alma-Marceau

 01-53-68-27-81

 25 frs. adults 26 and up,
20 frs. ages 12–25, 15
frs. children 5–11

 May–Sept, M–W and Sa–Su 11–5;
Oct–Apr, M–W and Sa–Su 11–4

 6 and up

Along the way, you discover that sewers are a fairly recent innovation for Paris. Up until the Middle Ages, the city got its drinking water from the Seine and disposed of its wastes in surrounding fields or by piping garbage and unmentionable refuse through narrow, open channels of packed earth called *ruelles* (a name many small streets still have). Around 1200, King Philippe-Auguste had many Parisian streets paved, with channels running down their middles to carry waste away. During Napoléon's time, underground sewers with arched ceilings were installed, but it wasn't until the 1850s, when Baron Haussmann overhauled the whole city by laying huge boulevards through it, that today's extensive sewer system began to take form. It's mind-boggling to think of how the city must have smelled until that time. You'll get a hint of it from the strong, je ne sais quoi smell permeating your tour.

HEY, KIDS! Which city has the world's biggest sewer system? No, it's not New York or Tokyo. It's Chicago! Paris's system is ranked the world's second largest. The visit lets you check out about 4,500 feet of it, a tiny part of the whole network.

KEEP IN MIND The tour takes an hour (not counting the time spent standing in line to get in), and people with claustrophobic tendencies may be uncomfortable. While you're in the neighborhood, you might want to visit Paris's Église Américaine (American Church; 65 quai d'Orsay, tel. 01–47–05–07–99). In addition to services, the church sponsors or hosts a number of public-service organizations, language classes, and activities for children and families. A bulletin board near the main desk has notices about activities and ads about jobs, things for sale, and other subjects of interest to Paris's expat American community.

FONDATION CLAUDE MONET

You can spend a day in the country and enjoy the arts, too, in Giverny, a pretty little village on the bank of the Seine west of Paris that was home to the Impressionist painter Claude Monet from 1883 to his death in 1926. Tops on the list is a visit to Monet's house, now a museum (but called the Claude Monet Foundation), which was saved from decay a few years ago by an international group of Monet fans. You'll get a feel for what life was like when the artist lived and worked here and made the house a gathering place for his artist friends. Coming here also lets kids who've seen Monet's water-lily paintings in the Musée d'Orsay (see below) make the connection between those works and the real person who created them in the nearby garden.

The first thing you'll notice is Monet's love of color. The house, set in a luxuriant garden, has peachy-pink walls and deep green shutters on the outside. On the inside, rooms have been restored as much as possible to what they were when Monet lived in them. Even

KID-FRIENDLY EATS **Les Nymphéas** (48 rue Claude-Monet, tel. 02–32–21–20–31) has good fixed-price menus, salads, and ice cream. The **Musée de l'Art Américain restaurant/tearoom** (see Keep in Mind) offers light meals and afternoon pastries; eat on the terrace and let the kids run in the garden.

KEEP IN MIND Another Giverny attraction, the Musée d'Art Américain (99 rue Claude-Monet, tel. 02– 32–51–94–65), in an elegant contemporary building, holds a permanent collection and changing exhibits of works by American artists with close ties to France. A booklet (in English) takes you on a fun tour. The museum also organizes arts conferences, concerts, and arts-related films (often in English). Through the very popular Ateliers en Plein Air (outdoor painting workshops), anyone over seven can join a small group (maximum 12) and paint in the museum's garden, getting feedback from English-speaking art instructors (reservations advised).

59 rue Claude-Monet, Giverny

02-32-51-28-21

35 frs. adults 26 and up, 25 frs. ages 12–25, 20 frs. children 6–11

Apr–Oct, T–Su 10–6

7 and up

small children should like the buttercup-yellow dining room with its big farmhouse table, yellow chimneypiece, and Monet's favorite Japanese prints on the walls. Renoir, Sisley, Cézanne, Manet, and Pissarro all came here to share the copious gourmet meals Monet favored, and to debate about art. Kids should like the cheery kitchen, too, which is filled with gorgeous bright-blue Portuguese tiles and more gleaming copper saucepans than you ever thought existed. You can also visit the painter's studio, furnished like a den with armchairs and little tables. There are no original paintings here now, but reproductions of Monet's works hang on the walls to remind you of the images that the artist created in this place.

Kids should enjoy a tour of the garden, with its paths winding through banks of flowers, its water-lily-filled ponds, and its picturesque Japanese bridge immortalized in Monet's works. You'll feel like you've walked inside one of his paintings.

TRANSPORTATION Giverny is 87 kilometers (54 miles) west of Paris. By rail, take the Rouen–Le Havre train from Paris's Gare Saint-Lazare and get off at the Vernon stop, from which you can take a taxi or bus to Giverny, around 3 miles (5 kilometers) away. You can also rent bicycles at the station in Vernon and bike to Giverny. From the train station, cross the bridge over the Seine and turn right. By car, take the A13 autoroute (toll highway) from Paris toward Le Havre, and get off at the Vernon exit. From Vernon, take the D191 and the D5 roads to Giverny.

FRANCE MINIATURE

I f you've ever wished you could visit all of France in a day, now you can. This theme park in a suburb 25 kilometers (16 miles) west of Paris contains more than 150 models of villages, monuments, and other sites from all over France, all carefully re-created at a scale of ⅟₃₀th the size of the originals. Everything has been done with an attention to detail that can only be described as obsessive.

The models stand on what's basically a big relief map of France, with every site placed exactly where it ought to be in relation to the others. Even the neighborhoods around each site have been reproduced, right down to the tiniest side street. The real trees and bushes here, 25,000 of them, have been trimmed to ⅟₃₀th their normal sizes, and the park's landscape designers have made sure that every miniaturized geographical feature represented—every hill, every river—is as accurate as possible. The Château de Versailles surrounded by its gardens looks exactly like the real thing, but smaller, with every turret, fountain, and statue reproduced in a 100-meter display.

TRANSPORTATION France Miniature is in the village of Elancourt, near St-Quentin-en-Yvelines, which is west of Paris near Versailles. By car, take the A13 highway west of Paris, then the A12 toward St-Quentin-en-Yvelines. Follow the signs to France Miniature. By rail from Paris's Gare Montparnasse, take the train to La Verrière; then follow the signs to the France Miniature bus (#411), which takes you to the park. A combined train–bus–park-entrance ticket for France Miniature is available at all Paris train stations.

25 rte. du Mesnil, Elancourt

08-36-68-53-35
www.franceminiature.com

 75 frs. ages 17 and up,
50 frs. children 4–16

Mar–Sept, daily 10–7
(July–Aug, Sa to 12 AM);
Oct–Nov, W–Th and Sa–Su 10–7

3 and up

It's certainly a little strange to see an Eiffel Tower whose first level you can reach out and touch while you're standing on the ground, but kids will love running around this Lilliputian world, picking out the monuments they recognize. Animated figures, taped sounds, and electronically controlled boats, trains, and cars bring the displays to life. Kids learn something here, too, because the park demonstrates not only France's geography and topography but also the country's great variety of architectural styles—from ancient to modern and region to region. Special events are regularly organized in the park, such as food fairs, regattas of remote-controlled boats, and big (not miniature) fireworks extravaganzas in summer.

KID-FRIENDLY EATS The theme park contains two restaurants, **La Poêlée** and **Les Provinces,** both serving traditional French dishes (normal size) and both with a choice of fixed-price and kids' menus. The park also has a picnic area if you'd like to bring your own goodies.

HEY, KIDS! France Miniature's models were created by a team of 53 architects and model-makers using real bricks, tile, and stone. The model of the Château de Chambord (in the Loire Valley) took 2,000 hours to build and cost 500,000 francs, and the model of the Stade de France, the stadium where France won the World Cup soccer title in 1998, contains 50,000 lifelike spectators, all painted by hand—and all to scale. The model of the Eiffel Tower was one of the most difficult to build and cost 1 million francs.

HALLE SAINT-PIERRE

Here's an innovative arts center for kids that parents also enjoy. Housed in a beautifully renovated 19th-century structure that once was a covered food market, the Halle Saint-Pierre is just off pretty Willette park, which slopes down the steep hillside under Sacre Coeur. Among its many offerings, the center has an exhibition space for temporary shows geared to children and families (one example comprised art that used recycled materials); one-hour *ateliers* (classes) for kids in dance, music, and art; a folk art museum; and other performances and programs of interest to artistically minded kids.

One of the main reasons the Halle Saint-Pierre is popular among Parisian families is the ateliers, which are held all year long on Wednesdays, Saturdays, and during school vacations from 2 to 3 (in French). Classes are usually geared to the special exhibits going on in the center at the time, and children are encouraged to show up an hour early to tour the exhibit before coming to class.

KID-FRIENDLY EATS The center's in-house **Café Halle Saint-Pierre** is a popular spot for snacks and drinks. French kids favor *grenadine*, a glass of bubbly water flavored with sweet, red fruit syrup. (You can also order coffee or a Coke.) See also Sacre Coeur and Montmartre.

HEY, KIDS! A special Halloween party for kids is held in the Halle Saint-Pierre every year, one sign that Halloween—which is not a traditional French holiday—has taken Paris by storm. The French have their own kind of Halloween, but it's celebrated very differently. It's called Toussaint (All Saints' Day), and it's on November 1. Toussaint is the day when everyone is supposed to remember people who have died, and in the past this meant visiting a cemetery. Until the last five years or so, most French kids hadn't even heard of trick-or-treating for candy.

2 rue Ronsard, 18e. Métro: Anvers

01–42–58–72–89
www.hallestpierre.org

 Center free; museum 40 frs. adults, 30 frs. children 17 and under, 45 frs. with kids' class

 M–Sa 10–6

 4 and up; ateliers 7–12

Also in the center, the kid-friendly Musée d'Art Naïf Max Fourny contains colorful works of folk art that appeal to even the smallest children. They'll laugh at the big painting of giant crabs pinching people with their huge claws and at the portrait of a troupe of musical monkeys. Guignol puppet shows and theatrical performances for kids (in French) are hosted on Wednesday, Saturday, and Sunday afternoons at 3:30 and 4:30, and special events are organized during Halloween, Christmas, and Easter.

The fun continues just outside the center in the place St-Pierre, a little square where you find a colorful antique merry-go-round and a kids' play area outfitted with a sandbox and climbing equipment. The funicular train that takes you up to Sacre Coeur (see Sacre Coeur and Montmartre) begins in this square.

KEEP IN MIND The children's ateliers are much in demand, so if your kids are interested in participating in one, it's best to call ahead to find out what's being offered and to reserve a place. If you also have children who are too young for the workshops, you can drop the older one off and spend the hour with the younger ones playing in the nearby park or taking them for a ride on the funicular.

HÔTEL NATIONAL DES INVALIDES

Topped with the glittering gold dome of the 17th-century Église du Dôme church, Les Invalides (as Parisians call it) originally housed a splendid hospital for invalid soldiers who'd served King Louis XIV. Today, this imposing complex of four elegant pavilions around a huge central courtyard is home to Napoléon's tomb (in the Église du Dôme, commissioned by Louis XIV as a church for visiting aristocracy), the adjoining Église St-Louis-des-Invalides (a smaller, very plain church designed for soldier-patients), and three museums containing largely military exhibits.

Kids should enjoy seeing the imposing blood-red tomb of the brilliant, power-hungry soldier who began his career calling himself a man of the people and eventually had himself named emperor. Exiled in 1815 after his defeat at Waterloo, Napoléon died in 1821. His body was returned to France for a grandiose funeral in 1840, but his tomb here wasn't ready until 1861. Today, Napoléon lies inside a set of coffins made of mahogany, tin, lead, ebony, and oak. He's not going anywhere.

KEEP IN MIND The Musée de l'Armée organizes a number of special activities for kids (in French). In *visites-contes* (visit-stories), children 7–12 and their families are taken around the collection and told entertaining stories about objects (Wednesday and Saturday at 2, 38 frs. adults, 30 frs. children). As part of an *armoiries et emblèmes* (coats of arms and shields) workshop, kids create their own personal crests using medieval symbols and colors. *Parcours-découvertes* (discovery map) brochures contain games and questions that help families see the collection in new ways. For information on kids' classes, call 01–44–42–51–73 (reservations advised).

Esp. des Invalides, 7e. Métro: Latour-Maubourg

01–45–55–37–72
www.invalides.org

38 frs. adults,
28 frs. ages 12–18

Apr–Sept, daily 10–5:45; Oct–Mar, daily
10–4:45; Napoléon's tomb mid-June–
mid-Sept, daily 10–6

7 and up

The Musée de l'Armée (Army Museum) has a vast collection of kid-pleasing weaponry and other military gear: intricate medieval weapons, a suit of armor worn by King Henri II when he was a child, early firearms from the time of Louis XIII, a war outfit once worn by the Emperor of China, medieval shields and heraldry, and, for a touch of the macabre, Napoléon's dog, stuffed, in the section of Napoléon memorabilia. The Musée des Plans-Reliefs—literally, a museum devoted to relief maps—is actually a collection of scale models of France's most famous fortified cities, complete with moats and drawbridges. In the Église St-Louis-des-Invalides, you see a set of flags French troops took from their enemies in 19th- and 20th-century battles. The Musée de l'Ordre de la Libération—which is devoted to World War II and especially to France's liberation from Nazi occupation—gives kids who've visited the Catacombes (see above), secret headquarters of the French Résistance, some background on that movement.

KID-FRIENDLY EATS The Musée de l'Armée has a **cafeteria. Le Pagode** (57 bis rue de Babylone, tel. 01–45–55–48–48) is a movie theater–tearoom in a Chinese pagoda. **The Real McCoy** (194 rue de Grenelle, tel. 01–45–56–98–82) has U.S.-style sandwiches. See also Musée Rodin and Tour Eiffel.

HEY, KIDS! You've probably never seen as many cannons as you'll find in the Musée de l'Armée; they're everywhere. Check out the beautifully decorated 18th-century ones in the central courtyard, one of which is named Le Maniac. If you look inside the barrels of the cannons, you'll see that they're carved in a spiral pattern. This caused the cannonball to spin when it was shot out of the barrel, which made it fly straighter and more accurately. Note the arrows on the cannons; they indicate which end the ball comes out, just in case some soldier got confused.

JARDIN D'ACCLIMATATION

Ready for a ride on a caterpillar? Want to see a puppet show, perform in a circus, and try out the latest interactive computer technology, all in one park? Then come to the Jardin d'Acclimatation, Paris's oldest children's amusement park, which has been pleasing kids and their families since 1860.

Though some attractions do look as if they've been here since the park first opened, all have been recently renovated. There's a little mini-farm where farm animals roam free; a petting zoo that's home to small, cuddly creatures like miniature goats; a hall of mirrors; and a sedate family of bears. Youngsters especially love these classics, which just goes to show that old-fashioned amusements can still have great kid appeal.

Moving into the 20th century, you have your choice of two roller coasters (the aforementioned caterpillar, for smaller kids, and a bigger, scarier coaster for bigger, fearless kids), an

HEY, KIDS!

Ever wanted to be a circus star? Now's your chance. In the morning you learn circus arts from the resident circus performers. Then you have lunch with them, and in the afternoon you perform with them under the big top. On with the show!

KID-FRIENDLY EATS

The park contains snack bars and three restaurants, two of which—**Le Pavillon des Oiseaux** (tel. 01–40–67–92–93) and **La Cheminée du Bowling** (tel. 01–53–64–93–02)—serve Sunday brunch. In Neuilly-sur-Seine, **Monoprix** (72 av. Charles-de-Gaulle, tel. 01–47– 45–24–42) department store sells picnic food, **Lina's Sandwiches** (156 av. Charles-de-Gaulle, tel. 01–47–45–24–42) has U.S.-style sandwiches and salads to eat in or take out, and **Durand Dupont Drugstore** (14 pl. du Marché, tel. 01–41–92–93–00) serves a copious Sunday brunch and great desserts anytime. See also Bois de Boulogne.

Bois de Boulogne, 16e. Métro: Porte
Maillot, Sablons

 14 frs. ages 3 and up;
some attractions extra

 June–Sept, daily 10–7;
Oct–May, daily 10–6; train,
circus, puppets W and Sa–Su

 01–40–67–90–82
www.jardindacclimatation.fr

9 months–12 yrs

extremely tame riverboat ride, very untame bumper cars and go-carts, a miniature golf course;
and fairground-type games. Children can even learn how to swing through the air on a flying
trapeze at the resident Cirque Diana Moreno Bormann, a small circus that gives classes and
puts on performances. In the Maison Enchantée, a fairy-tale environment that brings you
into the 21st century, older kids can play with high-tech gadgets, toddlers can swim in a
pool full of plastic balls, and babies nine months and up can roll around in an *espace mousse*
(foam room) just for them. Explor@drome has hands-on science displays and computer
games, and the Musée en Herbe (see below) is a special kids' museum. Activities for kids
four and up are organized in the Ateliers du Jardin.

Is it any wonder that after almost a century and a half, this 9-acre park is still going
strong, as are the running, jumping, playing kids who habitually pack it?

KEEP IN MIND: The most fun way to arrive at the Jardin d'Acclimatation is to take Le Petit Train from the Porte Maillot (at the edge of the
Bois de Boulogne) to the amusement park's entrance. The little steam engine–
powered train runs every 15 minutes (11–6) on Wednesday, Saturday, and Sunday and every day during school vacations. A 28 frs.-per-person round-trip
ticket includes park admission. If your kids are interested in the circus classes,
reserve in advance (tel. 01–45–00–23–01). Although they're in French,
they're based on actions, so non-French-speakers should cope.

JARDIN DE SCULPTURE EN PLEIN AIR

I n a little public park (Jardin Tino Rossi) next to a cobblestone quai on the Seine, Paris's open-air sculpture garden is one art display that kids won't be bored by. Officially it's called the Musée de la Sculpture en Plein Air de la Ville de Paris, but that's an awfully unwieldy name for one of the city's most accessible art venues. Here monumental sculptures created by some of the most famous artists of the 20th century (Brancusi, Zadkine, César) can be touched, climbed on, and generally treated like familiar objects. In fact, the whole point of this museum is that it doesn't feel like a museum at all. There are no barriers between you and the sculpture, and in fact no barriers between you and the Seine, so keep a close eye on toddlers.

The little park is long and narrow, with rambling, curving sidewalks kids like to skate or ride bikes on. There are lots of trees, flowers, and park benches, though as in most city

HEY, KIDS! From the sculpture garden, you can clearly see the so-called flying buttresses on the back of Notre-Dame. These 50-foot-tall stone arches were added to the cathedral in the 14th century to support its walls so that bigger stained-glass windows could be installed. The buttresses don't fly, of course, but in the 14th century, when this church was by far the tallest building in Paris, people must have thought that the soaring buttresses looked as if they might actually take off.

Quai St-Bernard, 5e, Métro: Austerlitz

 Free

Daily 24 hrs

08–36–68–31–12
Office de Tourisme

All ages

parks, you're not supposed to walk or sit on the grass. There's even a big children's play area, with climbing equipment and slides, that has a fence around it so little kids can't sneak out while their parents' backs are turned.

The sculpture garden is a favorite spot among Parisians for a Sunday stroll *en famille* before or after a visit to the nearby Jardin des Plantes. Musicians, joggers, and people pushing sleeping babies in strollers also hang out here, and several houseboats that have been made into living quarters are docked here permanently. On weekends, you'll often see a group of tango fanatics dancing in a paved area next to the river. A special plus is the spectacular view you'll have of Notre-Dame across the Seine, and you won't have to share it with a zillion tour buses.

KEEP IN MIND
Since this garden is accessible to anyone at any time, unsavory types sometimes hang out here at night. During the day, however, the park is constantly patrolled by guards, who, along with ensuring your safety, ensure the safety of the grass.

KID-FRIENDLY EATS
The park's guards don't mind if you picnic on a park bench. You can also cross the river behind Notre-Dame and head for the Ile St-Louis, where you can sample Paris's most famous ice cream at **Berthillon** (31 rue St-Louis-en-Ile, tel. 01–43–54–31–61). You can get a luscious cone to go or sit down in the shop's tearoom, through the door to the right of the take-out window. Try the *gianduja* (chocolate-hazelnut) ice cream. Yum! See also Cathédrale de Notre-Dame-de-Paris, Jardin des Plantes, and Muséum National d'Histoire Naturelle.

JARDIN DES HALLES

This kid-friendly park in the very center of Paris was created on the spot where the city's central open-air food market, Les Halles, stood for 800 years. That Les Halles, the vibrant and picturesque "belly of Paris," was moved out to the Paris suburb of Rungis in 1969. Its replacement stretches out in beautifully landscaped sections, with historic Église St-Eustache on its north side. Arched trellises remind Parisian old-timers of the iron arches that stood over the old marketplace, but there the nostalgia stops. This modern park lacks the scruffy charm of the old Les Halles. In its place, it has substituted lots of features kids enjoy.

Kids like the waterfall, which they can actually get wet in; a fenced-in grassy area just for toddlers and their families; two well-equipped, free play areas with jungle gyms and other climbing equipment; an Olympic-size public pool (in the underground shopping complex beneath the park); and one of Paris's oldest and loveliest merry-go-rounds. The drawback:

HEY, KIDS!

Parisian kids love to climb on the giant head-and-hand sculpture between the St-Eustache church and the Les Halles fountain, and the open square in front of the head is perfect for throwing a Frisbee. You can wade in a fountain here, too.

KID-FRIENDLY EATS
Chicago Meatpackers (8 rue Coquillière, tel. 01–40–28–02–33) is a top choice when you just have to have a cheeseburger and home-made fries. An electric train circles above your heads, kids get balloons and coloring books, and there's entertainment at lunch. Treat the family to delicious Paris ice cream or take-out food at **Stohrer** (51 rue Montorgueil, tel. 01–42–33–38–20), a pastry shop that's been tempting Parisians since 1730; it's on a lively market street. For U.S.-style ice cream, try **Tom and Jerry's** (4 rue Pierre-Lescot, tel. 01–53–40–96–92) or **Häagen-Dazs** (Porte St-Eustache, tel. 01–42–36–15–31).

105 rue Rambuteau, 1er. Métro:
Les Halles

01-45-08-07-18

Free; Jardin des
Enfants 3½ frs.

Daily 24 hrs.; Jardin des Enfants T and Th–F 9–
12 and 2–6 plus Apr–June and Sept–Oct, W and
Sa–Su 10–6 (July–Aug, 10–7; Nov–Mar, 10–4)

3–12; Jardin
des Enfants 7–12

Unsavory characters hang out here, especially at night. The park is very well patrolled, however.

Le Jardin des Enfants des Halles is a small but special park for schoolchildren (7–12) in a corner of the Jardin des Halles. Unlike other Paris children's parks, this one is off-limits to parents, except on Sundays. Friendly trained staff help kids discover six different "worlds" within the little park: the *monde sauvage* (wild world), with canyons, waterfalls, and tiger traps; the *monde volcanique* (volcanic world), where kids can climb up the face of a small artificial volcano, down into its crater, and onto a mysterious island surrounded by water; the *monde mou* (soft world), with a ball crawl to swim in; the *monde géométrique et sonore* (world of geometry and sounds), where scientific experiments deal with numbers and sounds; and the *cité perdue* (lost city), where kids clamber through a labyrinth and into a giant snail.

KEEP IN MIND Kids are allowed to stay in the Jardin des Enfants des Halles for only one hour, and parents and children under 7 (with a parent) are only allowed in between 10 and 1 on Sundays. At other times, young children can call the open play area just in front of the entrance their own. The Forum des Images (tel. 01–44–76–62–00), in the Forum des Halles underground shopping mall, shows films for kids (in French) Wednesdays and Saturdays at 3; snacks are served after the film.

JARDIN DES PLANTES

Paris's historic botanical garden was first opened to the public in 1650, and from that time on it's been drawing families in search of a little nature in the city. Wide graveled walkways leading from the Seine to the Muséum National d'Histoire Naturelle complex are bordered by thousands of flowers and plants that look beautiful year-round. Sitting on a bench and watching the world go by is one of Paris's great free pleasures.

Kids can run off steam along the central garden's wide paths, and a fun children's play area (on the garden's western edge, near the rue Cuvier) has lots of structures to climb on, including a huge jungle-gym contraption that looks like a dinosaur. On the garden's southwestern edge, winding paths to the summit of a hill form a maze; older kids love to explore these little paths and will quickly get out of your sight if you're not careful.

The Jardin des Plantes contains the world's oldest public zoo, La Ménagerie, opened in 1794. Kids can see bears, giraffes, lions, orangutans, dozens of monkeys and birds, a variety

KID-FRIENDLY EATS There are several **snacks stands** near the zoo entrance as well as the **Restaurant de La Ménagerie,** whose specialty is crêpes, inside the zoo. **La Mosquée de Paris** (39 rue Geoffroy-St-Hilaire, tel. 01–43–31–18–14), adjoining Paris's gleaming white mosque, is a standout for mint tea and pastries in the tearoom or couscous (North African stew) in the restaurant. Try the *cornes de gazelle* (gazelle's horn) pastry. Among many small restaurants on the rue Linné, cozy **L'Écureuil** (3 rue Linné, tel. 01–43–31–61–18) serves garlicky southwestern French cooking. See also Muséum National d'Histoire Naturelle.

57 rue Cuvier, quai St-Bernard,
5e. Métro: Pl. Monge

 01-40-79-30-00 Muséum
National d'Histoire Naturelle

Gardens free; Grande
Serre 15 frs.; Ménagerie
30 frs. ages 17 and up,
20 frs. children 4–16

Gardens daily 7:30–sunset; Ménagerie
June–Sept, M–Sa 9–6, Su 9–6:30;
Oct–May, M–Sa 9–5, Su 9–6:30

All ages

of snakes, and even a few giant turtles. All the animals look well cared for, but their cages are small. This means kids can get a close-up look at them, but the animals themselves look bored and unhappy. The Microzoo (for kids 10 and up), within the main zoo, is filled with microscopes through which kids can check out microscopic animal life, including all the little creatures that live on a piece of cheese (not recommended just before lunch).

Nature-loving kids like checking out a tree that's supposedly the oldest in Paris, a faux acacia planted in 1636; it's on the allée des Becquerel. The Grande Serre (Great Greenhouse) nearby is so full of hothouse plants gone wild that going inside it is like a trip to the tropics (warning: it's closed Tuesdays). Kids can climb on the big rock at the back of the greenhouse to get a great view of this real urban jungle.

HEY, KIDS! The zoo's first elephant arrived in 1795, followed by the first bear, Martin. Ever since, all the zoo's bears have been named Martin in his honor. The zoo's first giraffe, Zarafa, sailed from Africa to Marseilles in 1827 and then walked to Paris.

KEEP IN MIND Kids *really* interested in plants will like the École de Botanique, with thousands of rare plants, and the Jardin Alpin, with plants from mountainous regions all over the world; both these gardens are within the main garden near the zoo. Note that the Jardin des Plantes is not always clean, especially in the woodsy section where the maze is located.

JARDIN DES TUILERIES

39

Thanks to its wide gravel walks, placid fountains, lawns—all with *pelouse interdite* (keep off the grass) signs— and carefully manicured flower beds stretching between the Louvre and the place de la Concorde, the Jardin des Tuileries is without a doubt the city's most elegant park. For generations, Parisian families have come here for outings. Parents relax on park benches while kids run around or, best of all, sail little boats on one of the park's ponds. (You rent a boat and a long pole from a stand set up next to the pond, hope your kids' boat will be one of the ones whose sails catch the wind, and encourage your children to use the pole to prod their craft away from the side of the pond if it gets stuck.)

This formal park had very humble beginnings: In the 15th century it was a quarry for clay that was used in making *tuiles* (roof tiles), the source of the park's name. Marie de Medici

KEEP IN MIND

The little sailboats are available for rent on Wednesdays, weekends, and school holidays. Excellent 90-minute workshops in art and gardening (in French) for kids 4–12 are organized in the Tuileries by an association called L'Enfance de l'Art (tel. 01–42–96–19–33).

KID-FRIENDLY EATS

There are **snack bars** and **drinks stands** scattered around the Tuileries. **Café Véry** (tel. 01–47–03–94–84)—chic, reasonably priced, and right in the middle of the park—has a good kids' menu and inventive light meals. You can also come here just for a pastry and sit indoors or out. **Angelina** (226 rue de Rivoli, tel. 01–42–60–82–00), a tearoom founded in 1903, has to-die-for hot chocolate and excellent (though pricey) pastries; kids must be on their best behavior. You'll see some very well-dressed Parisian families here. See also Musée du Louvre and Jardins du Palais-Royal.

Between pl. de la Concorde and the Louvre, 1er. Métro: Tuileries, Louvre

 Free

01-40-20-90-43

Apr–June and Sept, daily 7 AM–9 PM; July–Aug, M–F 7 AM–11:45 PM, Sa–Su 7 AM–1:45 AM; Oct–Mar, daily 7 AM–7:30 PM

 All ages

had the idea of creating an elegant, Italian-style garden here, and later the park was embellished by André Le Nôtre, the great garden designer responsible for the park around the Château de Versailles.

Today, the Tuileries contains many attractions for kids. There's a spacious, shady kids' play area with a sandbox and climbing equipment, a merry-go-round, sleepy little ponies to ride (though this tends to bore anyone over 7, since the ponies are led in a group), a Guignol puppet theater, special paths for skateboarders and rollerbladers, a trampoline, and even an open-air ice-skating rink in winter. In July and August and at Christmas, an enormous, garish carnival is set up, complete with a zillion stands where you can try your luck at various games, a roller-coaster ride, and a huge—REALLY huge—Ferris wheel. Kids love it, but it's a good thing Marie de Medici and Le Nôtre aren't around to see this.

HEY, KIDS! The Tuileries has seen a lot of world firsts: the first public toilets (in the 18th century), the first newspaper stand, and the first flight of a hot-air balloon, a 20-minute trip above Paris made by the Montgolfier brothers in 1783. Just a few years after that, in 1791, King Louis XVI and Marie-Antoinette tried to escape revolutionary mobs by fleeing across the Tuileries, but they were caught and thrown into prison and later guillotined on the nearby place de la Concorde.

JARDIN DU LUXEMBOURG

The Jardin du Luxembourg has been the city's favorite park for generations. This oh-so-Parisian park has it all: a beautiful palace, designed in 1615 and now the home of the French Sénat; huge trees; ponies to ride; tennis courts; beehives; the Grand Bassin pond, where kids can sail boats; and even—rarest of all in Paris—an area where you can actually walk on the grass (if you're accompanied by a toddler). One of the park's treasures is its merry-go-round, whose much-loved wooden animals were designed by none other than Charles Garnier, the 19th-century architect of the Paris Opéra. Next to the merry-go-round is the park's own puppet theater, the city's biggest (see Marionnettes du Luxembourg).

You'll find a special fenced-in kids' play area with its own admission charge in the southeast corner of the park, next to the puppet theater. It's kept spotlessly clean (not always the case in Paris parks) and filled with all sorts of structures kids can climb on,

KID-FRIENDLY EATS In the park's center, **La Buvette des Marionnettes du Luxembourg** (tel. 01–43–26–33– 04) serves drinks, sandwiches, crêpes, and ice cream. Don't expect gourmet goodies, but it's quick and there are tables outside. If your kids just have to have American-style burgers, there's a **McDonald's** (65 bd. St-Michel, tel. 01–46–33–02–08) nearby. Friendly **Pâtisserie Viennoise** (8 rue de l'École de Médecine, tel. 01–43– 26–60–48), a student hangout, has yummy *tourte salée* (quiche with a top crust), pâté, salads, hot chocolate, fresh fruit juices, and luscious pastries, all at rock-bottom prices; it's closed weekends, unfortunately. See also Marionnettes du Luxembourg.

Entrances: rue de Medicis, rue Guynemer, bd. St-Michel, rue de Vaugirard, 6e. Métro: Odéon. RER: Luxembourg

08-36-68-31-12
Office de Tourisme

Free, some attractions charge

Apr–Oct., daily 7–sunset; Nov–Mar, daily 8–sunset

All ages

swing down, swirl through the air on, or simply sit in. Toddlers love the sandbox, and bigger kids with an urge to climb gravitate toward a tall spider-web contraption that looks a little like the Eiffel Tower.

Chess players congregate in front of the glass-walled Orangerie, which has a free play area for small children in front of it. In the middle of the park, you'll find some placid ponies that little kids stand in line to take a short ride on. Children in the mood for more action like the pedal-powered cars that operate near the park's southern edge. You can join the joggers along a popular circuit around the park, toss bits of baguette to resident pigeons, or, best of all, sit down in one of the park's distinctive pale-green metal chairs, listen to Parisians chattering around you, and realize you're really, truly in Paris.

KEEP IN MIND

If you take the kids to the fenced-in play area (highly recommended) and want to leave it—to see a puppet show, for example—but come back later, be sure to get your hands stamped at the desk on your way out.

HEY, KIDS! If you want to try your luck catching brass rings on the merry-go-round, choose a mount in the outer circle of animals (the ones closest to the edge). An attendant will hand you a stick. As the merry-go-round begins to turn, try to get your stick through the middle of the ring hanging down from a post. If you do it right (hint: keep the stick straight), the ring will fall off onto your stick, and the attendant will put a new ring on the post for the next child. (Give your rings back after the ride.)

JARDINS DU PALAIS-ROYAL

The Jardins du Palais-Royal are one of Paris's best-kept secrets, even though they're right in the middle of the most touristed part of the city (just a short walk from the Louvre). Almost always overlooked by visitors, this lovely little park surrounded by elegant 18th-century buildings (the writer Colette lived in one of them) is hard to find. You get to it by going through small passageways that you could walk right past and not see.

The park has long gravel walkways, shady trees, magnificently planted flower beds, lots of park benches, and—most special of all—hardly any traffic noise, because the buildings all around it block out the sound of the cars roaring by just a few yards away. Although it looks very formal, the park is popular among Parisian families, especially ones with smaller kids, since they can run around safe from traffic.

Toddlers can practice taking steps from park bench to park bench or play in the sandbox at the north end of the park, while bigger kids can kick a soccer ball or just play around

KEEP IN MIND Elegant shops under the surrounding arcades include La Boutique du Palais-Royal (9 rue Beaujolais, tel. 01–42–60–08–22), selling handmade wooden toys and other creative treats for kids. The astronomically priced toy soldiers in the antiques stores here are strictly for collectors.

KID-FRIENDLY EATS The ideally located **Salon du Thé du Palais-Royal** (tel. 01–40–20–00–27) has tables in the garden. **Cafés et Thés Verlet** (256 rue St-Honoré, tel. 01–42–60–67–39) is a cozy tearoom with excellent tea, coffee, sandwiches, and pastries. **A Priori Thé** (35–37 Galerie Vivienne, 66 rue Vivienne, tel. 01–42–97–48–75) is a tearoom with American-style treats and a great location under the glass roof of the Galerie Vivienne, an elegant early version of a shopping mall. See also Jardin des Tuileries and Musée du Louvre.

Entrances: off pl. André-Malraux, rue Beaujo-lais, rue de Valois, 1er. Métro: Palais-Royal

 Free

 Apr–May and Sept, daily 7:30 AM–10 PM; June–Aug, daily 7:30 AM–11 PM; Oct–Mar, daily 7:30 AM–8:30 PM

08-36-68-31-12 Office de Tourisme

All ages

on the artworks at the south end of the park. One of these, an installation by architect Daniel Buren, caused a controversy when it was built—its contemporary style in sharp contrast to the 18th-century structures around it—but kids love it. It's a wide expanse of pavement with water flowing under it, visible through grids; punctuating it are a series of columns kids can climb on and rows of little red lights in the pavement that make it look like a miniature landing strip. Don't forget to toss a coin into the pool near the columns; it's a Paris tradition. Among the other public art here is a fountain with shiny silver balls, created by Pol Bury. All around the fountain is a flat, paved area where little kids practice their roller-skating skills and supremely talented skateboarders sometimes show off their stuff. Kids might not know it's art, but they'll know they like it.

HEY, KIDS! If you're in this park at noon on Saturday, don't be surprised if you hear a loud BOOM. It's the Palais-Royal cannon. This little cannon, in a flower bed near the south end of the park, boomed at noon every day from 1786 to 1914—at least, when there was enough sun. The firing mechanism was activated by the heat of sun shining through a magnifying glass at a precise angle so that it would set off a small charge of gunpowder precisely at midday. The cannon was restored a few years ago, and now its firing mechanism is automatic.

MARIONNETTES DU LUXEMBOURG

There are puppet theaters all over Paris, but the city's biggest and one of its best is in the middle of the Jardin du Luxembourg (see above). It's the Marionnettes du Luxembourg, and the classic puppet shows staged here are bound to please your kids whether or not they speak French.

Opened in 1933 by the Desarthis family and still run by them, the puppet theater is housed in a nondescript building in the middle of the park, next to the merry-go-round and near the fenced-in play area. Before each show, staff members ring a bell outside the theater to let you know it's time to stand in line.

The shows change regularly, but all feature the classic French puppet hero Guignol, who has been around since at least the 18th century, when he was cast as a bloodthirsty villain. Today, Guignol is definitely the good guy. He's the character with a long black pigtail wearing a long Chinese-style coat, but you won't have to look for him, because as soon as he appears

KEEP IN MIND Other good Parisian puppet theaters are the Guignol du Jardin d'Acclimatation, in the Bois de Boulogne (16e); the Marionnettes du Champ de Mars, near the Eiffel Tower (7e); the Marionnettes des Champs-Élysées, in the Jardin des Champs-Élysées (8e); the Guignol de Paris, in the Parc des Buttes Chaumont (19e); and the Marionnettes du Parc Georges Brassens (15e). Performances at all of them are given on Wednesday, Saturday, and Sunday afternoons and more often during school vacations. See individual listings for several of these parks.

Jardin du Luxembourg, 6e.
Métro: Odéon, RER: Luxembourg

 01-43-26-46-47

 24 frs.

 W and Sa–Su 3 (sometimes 2 shows)

4 and up

on stage every French kid in the audience will shriek his name. Guignol has a good heart but is constantly getting into trouble, usually by trying to help out one of his neighbors in the generic French village (or Paris neighborhood) where he lives. As Guignol stumbles blindly into one disaster after another, kids scream advice to him, warn him about the bad guys, and in general try to help him, but no matter what they do, Guignol is bound to get his head whacked more than once. Your children should have no problem getting the gist of the story. At intermission, the curtain is closed and kids crowd around the front of the stage, where nice ladies sell candy.

Thankfully, Guignol always manages to emerge unscathed, and at the end of each show, he takes a few bows and tells the audience to come back again soon. Your kids will no doubt be happy to do just that.

HEY, KIDS! When you enter the theater, leave your parents behind and go sit as close to the stage as possible to get a good look at the action (and the puppets, which are bigger than you might think). The front rows are for kids only.

KID-FRIENDLY EATS Pâtisserie Dalloyau (2 pl. Edmund-Rostand, tel. 01–43–29–31–10) has delicious pastries as well as quiches and sandwiches that you can take out or sample in the store's elegant in-house tearoom. Well-dressed Parisian moms and grandmothers bring their equally well-dressed, well-behaved children here for a treat after a stroll in the park. The casual **La Buvette des Marionnettes du Luxembourg** (tel. 01–43–26–33–04), next to the theater, has drinks, snacks, light meals, and ice cream. See also Jardin du Luxembourg.

MÉDAILLONS D'ARAGO

35

P aris is filled with monuments to France's native sons and daughters, but there's one you could easily miss. In fact, you could step on it and not see it, and finding it is a treasure hunt kids should enjoy. The monument honors Dominique Arago (1786–1853), an astronomer and physicist who made major contributions to the early study of electromagnetism and who patriotically championed the Paris meridian (the longitude line that passes through the city) as the international mean-time line. France and Ireland actually kept to French mean time until 1911, when both countries joined the world in adopting Greenwich mean time.

In honor of Arago's achievements, France erected a bronze statue of him that once stood on the boulevard Arago (also named for him), but the German army melted the statue down during World War II. Then in 1995 Arago was again honored, this time with a most unusual monument: a series of 135 bronze *médaillons* (disks)—each 12 centimeters (4½ inches) in diameter and marked simply with the name Arago—implanted in pavement

HEY, KIDS!

One good spot to find Arago is on the quai Malaquais (métro: St-Germain-des-Prés), across the Seine from the Louvre. Walk west along the quai from where the Passerelle des Arts pedestrian bridge meets the Left Bank, keeping your eyes peeled for a disk.

KID-FRIENDLY EATS

Near the observatory, **Contre-Allée** (83 av. Denfert-Rochereau, tel. 01–43–54–99– 86) is a bistro offering generous servings of classic French cooking, though it's not cheap. Colorful rue Daguerre is lined with restaurants and food shops, including **Le Moulin de la Vièrge** (82 rue Daguerre, tel. 01–45–43–09– 84), for delicious breads (try the sourdough *pain au levain*) and pastries. See also Catacombes and Jardin du Luxembourg. If you're hunting on the quai Malaquais, look under the Musée d'Orsay for suggestions, or take along a picnic to share with the ducks that hang out on the quai.

Sq. Ile de Seine, 98 bd. Arago, 14e to Montmartre library, 18 av.
Pte-de-Montmartre, 18e. Métro: Denfert-Rochereau, St-Jacques,
Porte de Clignancourt

Free

Daily 24 hrs

4 and up

08–36–68–31–12 Office de Tourisme

several meters apart along the Paris meridian line. The line of disks (some of which have been stolen) begins where the Arago statue once stood, on the boulevard Arago facing the gardens of the Observatoire de Paris (Paris Observatory).

It passes through the Jardin du Luxembourg, the quai Malaquais, the Jardin des Tuileries, and the Jardins du Palais-Royal (see listings) before ending on the city's northern edge, in front of the Bibliothèque de la Porte de Montmartre (Montmartre's public library). The observatory, where Arago once worked, has been a center for the study of time and the stars since it was built in 1667. Its south wall is on Paris's latitude line (48°50'), and the Paris meridian passes right through it, so naturally a few Arago disks are in the observatory and its garden (observatory closed to visitors; garden open May–October). To go on a treasure hunt, start in the square Ile de Sein, in the observatory garden, or anywhere along the Paris meridian, and look out for Arago under your feet.

KEEP IN MIND The detailed Institut Géographique National (IGN) map of Paris, sold at most Paris bookstores and *maisons de presse* (newspaper shops), shows the meridian line. If you search for Arago on the quai Malaquais, remember that Paris quais do not have barriers along the Seine. Keep the kids away from the edge!

MUSÉE DE LA CONTREFAÇON

Will the real Barbie please stand up? That may be the only way you can figure out which one she is, without the help of this quirky little museum devoted to exposing trickery. Its name means the Museum of Counterfeits, and it exhibits fake Hermès scarves, fake Louis Vuitton bags with the famous "LV" logo, and, more interesting to kids, fake Legos, fake computer games, fake running shoes, and lots of fake toys, all displayed next to genuine originals. There are about 400 items in all, proof that nothing is safe from the counterfeiter.

The counterfeits here really do run the gamut. There's a bunch of Barbie dolls that look almost exactly, but not quite, like a real Barbie, and a coffeemaker that *does* look exactly like the real thing, only with a different brand name. Some fakes look pretty, well, fakey, while others look so much like the originals that you can understand how so many people get taken in by high-priced counterfeit goods every year. That's why the Union des Fabricants, a French manufacturer's organization, set up this museum: to show people how

KID-FRIENDLY EATS **Pâtisserie Alsacienne** (91 av. Raymond-Poincaré, tel. 01–45–00–56–55) has yummy quiches, *kougelhopf* (brioche-type bread with candied fruits), strudel, and *gâteau forêt-noire* (Black Forest cake). **Lillo** (35 rue des Belles-Feuilles, tel. 01–47–27–69–08) is one of Paris's top cheese stores. Try the kid-pleasing *comté* or various take-out items made with cheese, like *gougères* (cheesy cream puffs) or the *feuilleté de roquefort* (cheese-filled puff pastry). Reliable **Bistro Romain** (6 pl. Victor-Hugo, tel. 01–45–00– 65–03) has a good kids' menu (lasagna or hamburger and fries) and all-you-can-eat chocolate mousse. See also Bois de Boulogne.

16 rue de la Faisanderie, 16e. Métro: Porte Dauphine

 01-56-26-14-00
www.unifab.com

 15 frs. ages 12 and up

T-Sa 2-5:30

 10 and up

widespread counterfeiting is and what problems it can cause. One display shows how counterfeits can rip off both the original producer of an item and the consumer, who might get an inferior product. Another demonstrates how fake toys, appliances, and industrial parts can actually be very dangerous, and yet another reveals that cheap counterfeit goods bought abroad may turn out not to be a bargain after all, since they are often confiscated by savvy customs officials. Historical objects, such as a counterfeit Gallo-Roman amphora created centuries ago (and donated to the museum by Jacques Cousteau), show that counterfeiting has been around for a very long time.

There's nothing hands-on in this museum, but kids should have fun trying to pick out the details that make the fakes different from the real things, and older kids are usually intrigued by the moral issues of counterfeiting that this museum brings to their attention.

HEY, KIDS! Things aren't always what they seem, and one such thing is the building this museum is in. It looks just like an 18th-century Parisian townhouse, but it isn't. It was built in authentic 18th-century style, all right, but it was built a century later, in the late 19th century, in imitation of a certain 18th-century mansion in the Marais district, on the other side of town. That mansion has since been torn down, but this fake is still here. The moral of the story: Sometimes fakes outlive the originals.

KEEP IN MIND

This museum could make a fun side trip from the nearby Bois de Boulogne (see above), especially since the entrance fee is so low. It's also a nice excuse for a little French lesson: "counterfeit" comes from the French words *contre* ("against") and *fait* ("made").

MUSÉE DE LA CURIOSITÉ ET DE LA MAGIE

33

A ny kid (or grown-up) who has ever tried to perform magic tricks is bound to be enthralled by this very unusual museum housed in ancient vaulted cellars in the heart of the historic Marais district. Visitors set out on a journey into the world of illusion, their senses on the alert as they try to separate truth from falsehood. It's not easy. You see strange animated objects, test your perceptions with interactive optical illusions, learn the secrets of bizarre scientific equipment, and check out various tools of the magician's trade. The really original feature of this museum is that its staff members are all trained magicians. They act as your guides throughout your visit, performing magic tricks to show you their craft in action.

This is museum as performance space, and audience participation is part of the show. You see conjuring tricks, sleight-of-hand card tricks, and other thought-teasers that have

HEY, KIDS!

Have you ever heard of the English expression "legerdemain"? It comes from the French words for "light" (*leger*), "of" (*de*), and "hand" (*main*), or in other words, sleight-of-hand. The French don't use this expression, though. When they mean "legerdemain," they say *prestidigitation*. Go figure!

KID-FRIENDLY EATS Two excellent tearooms are **Le Loir dans la Théière** (3 rue des Rosiers, tel. 01–42–72–68–12), with scrumptious snacks in an Alice-in-Wonderland atmosphere, and **Marais Plus** (20 rue des Francs-Bourgeois, tel. 01–48–87–01–40), adjoining a toy shop. Friendly **Le Petit Bofinger** (6 rue de la Bastille, tel. 01–42–72–05–23), a bistro branch of a chic brasserie, has good fixed-price menus. For picnic goods, try the food shops on the rue St-Antoine. For breads, don't miss the *baguette à l'ancienne* or the olive *fougasse* at **Malineau** (26 rue St-Paul, tel. 01–43–54–97–15). See also Musée Picasso and Place des Vosges and the Marais.

attracted audiences to magic shows for centuries. (Everything is in French, but staff members are usually able to make explanations in English, if necessary; gestures can go a long way, too.) The enthusiastic guides are very good at getting kids involved in the act and try to give every child a chance to participate at some point. You're also given time to conduct your own experiments with the interactive equipment.

On Saturdays the museum operates the École de Magie (School of Magic), open to anyone 12 or older, adults included. You can choose a morning or afternoon class, with mornings concentrating on card tricks and afternoons devoted to other kinds of magic tricks. (These classes, too, are in French.) You and your whole family can emerge not only amazed by what you see but also ready to wow your friends with your own feats of illusion.

KEEP IN MIND The École de Magie is a popular family activity, so it's best to check on opening times and reserve in advance if you'd like to participate. After your visit to the museum, you might want to take a look at the nearby Magasin de Magie store (13 rue du Temple, tel. 01-42-74-06-74). Here you can stock up on magic wands, boxes with secret compartments, decks of trick cards, and even videos (in French) showing you how to perform various magic tricks.

MUSÉE DE L'AIR ET DE L'ESPACE

For anyone who loves airplanes, this air and space museum is a must. It's housed in the historic Aéroport Le Bourget, the former main city airport. If the name sounds familiar, it's because aviator Charles Lindbergh landed his *Spirit of St. Louis* here in May 1927, becoming the first person to complete a transatlantic flight. What you may not know is that 13 days earlier, pilots Charles Nungesser and François Coli took off from Le Bourget in an attempt to do the same—but disappeared. You can learn about this and other aviation history at this vast exhibition space, which occupies the former main terminal and part of a runway and showcases air travel from 1879 to the present.

The Prototypes 1945–1970 et l'Armée de l'Air exhibit contains prototypes and military aircraft, and Entre Deux Guerres displays light aircraft and stunt planes from 1920 to 1970, with a concentration on nonmilitary aircraft from the 1920s and 1930s (the period between the two world wars that the exhibit name implies). The Hall de l'Espace has models of satellites, including *Sputnik 57,* and of *Apollo 13,* and in the Hall Concorde you can climb aboard the

KEEP IN MIND Kids who aren't thrilled by airplanes, as well as younger children (6 and under), may soon tire of viewing plane after plane in vast hangars and exhibition spaces, especially since there's a lot of walking involved. If you think that might be a problem, limit your visit to the top kid-pleasers: the Grande Galerie, where the rarest and earliest aircraft are displayed, and the Hall Concorde, where kids can get inside a Concorde. In mid-June in odd-numbered years, Le Bourget airport hosts the huge Paris air show (official name: Salon Internationale de l'Aéronautique et de l'Espace).

Aéroport Le Bourget, Le Bourget

 40 frs. ages 17 and up, 30 frs. children 8–16

May–Oct, M and W–Su 10–6; Nov–Apr, M and W–Su, 10–5

 01-49-92-71-99
www.mae.org

 7 and up

prototype for the first Concorde and see famous planes flown during World War II (e.g., Spitfire, Mustang).

The Grande Galerie includes aviation instruments and equipment from the earliest days of flying machines, along with a superb collection of early aircraft (1879–1918). You can see the passenger section of the 1884 *La France* dirigible, along with the world's first glider (1879), a 1906 Vuia plane, and Henri Fabre's 1910 *hydraplane*. Looking at these tiny, fragile-looking constructions makes you appreciate the courage of those who dared take to the skies in them. Outside on the runway, you can check out combat planes, rocket launchers, two Ariane rockets, and a Concorde.

Half of the museum's visitors are school-age kids, most of whom come on field trips. To help them get the most out of their visit, the museum has prepared brochures (in French) that teach about the collection through games and stories.

KID-FRIENDLY EATS The airport does have a café, **Eurobar** (tel. 01–48–35–98–88). However, except during such special events as the Paris air show, when many food stands operate, there isn't a big choice. Better to snack while you're here and save your restaurant outing for later.

TRANSPORTATION By car or taxi, take the A1 highway north of Paris to the Aérogare Le Bourget exit (around 8 kilometers/5 miles). By public transport, take the métro to the La Courneuve–8 Mai stop, or take the RER commuter train (line B) from the center of Paris to Le Bourget, which is a stop on the train to Aéroport Roissy-Charles-de-Gaulle. From outside the entrance of either the métro or the RER station, take the number 152 bus to Aérogare Le Bourget. The trip by public transportation should take around 30 minutes, depending on train and bus connections.

MUSÉE DES ARTS ET MÉTIERS

The Musée des Arts et Métiers (Arts and Crafts Museum) would be better called the Museum of Inventions. Why? Because it doesn't showcase arts and crafts at all, but rather all sorts of technical innovations made from the 16th century to our own day. It's a place of inspiration for the world's next Leonardo da Vincis, and those who nurture and admire them.

The museum is housed in a spectacular building: the medieval abbey of St-Martin-des-Champs, which was completely renovated in a three-year project that brought it into the 21st century. Containing over 80,000 objects and documents, it illustrates groundbreaking, world-changing discoveries in the fields of physics, optics, mechanics, telecommunications, and more. Among these testaments to human creativity are everything from weird 18th-century versions of robots to the first movie cameras, invented by brothers Auguste-Marie and Louis-Jean Lumière in the late 19th century. One of the museum's prize objects—displayed in the abbey's former chapel, just to show you where this museum's heart

KEEP IN MIND One drawback to this museum is that it is much less hands-on than other Paris museums dedicated to scientific accomplishments. Smaller kids would probably be bored here, but the over-7 crowd should love looking at the planes, the pendulum, and other strange objects.

HEY, KIDS! *Star Wars* would never have been possible without the Lumière brothers (or someone like them). These aptly named men (*lumière* means "light") invented the world's first movie camera, made the world's first movies, and opened the world's first movie theater. Their first film wouldn't win an Academy Award; it showed workers leaving their factory. However, the second one, *L'Arroseur Arrosé* (*The Waterer Gets Watered*) could still make you laugh. The first-ever fiction film, it wasn't as impressive as a Skywalker saga, but hey, it was made more than a century ago.

292 rue St-Martin, 3e.
Métro: Arts-et-Métiers

 01–53–01–82–00
www.cnam.fr

 35 frs. adults 19 and up,
25 frs. ages 5–18

 T–W and F–Su 10–6, Th 10–9:30

7 and up

is—is a little 24-horsepower monoplane built by the French inventor and flyer Louis Blériot, who used it to become the first person to fly over the English Channel, in 1909.

Items from the 20th century include some equipment with which kids can do their own experiments with sound. The museum's most stunning object, though, is without a doubt the two-story pendulum created by the French physicist Jean-Bernard-Léon Foucault (1819–1868). Among his many inventions, which included the gyroscope and the first polarizer, Foucault used a pendulum to demonstrate that the earth rotates once a day. As Foucault's huge pendulum swings silently back and forth in a vast room, seemingly operated by unseen giants, it gives kids graphic proof that we are really swirling around in space.

KID-FRIENDLY EATS A nearby spot for a park-bench picnic is the shady square du Temple, which also has a kids' play area. **Léon de Bruxelles** (8 pl. de la République, tel. 01–43–38–25–19), a chain famous for its mussels, has one of the cheapest kids' menus in Paris, along with good fries. (Don't worry: You can choose a hamburger instead of mussels.) **À la Mexicaine** (68 rue Quincampoix, tel. 01–48–87–99–34) has Mexican (not Tex-Mex) dishes like *mole poblano* (stew with chocolate in the sauce), homemade tortillas, and a good kids' menu.

MUSÉE D'ORSAY

The vast Musée d'Orsay, a turn-of-the-last-century railway station imaginatively redesigned by architect Gae Aulenti, still bears marks of its past life, such as the great clock on the Seine-facing facade. (Once inside the museum, kids like checking out its workings from the back.) The museum showcases works created from 1848 to 1914, when Paris was recognized as the world's arts capital. Parents may come primarily for the Impressionist paintings, but kids like the wide variety of objects—from tiny, very early photographs of Paris to gigantic sculpture—presented in a vast, high-ceilinged space with lots of elbow room.

The Musée d'Orsay deserves kudos for making its collection accessible to younger visitors. Pick up a free art-quiz pamphlet, "Carnets Parcours Familles" (available in English), when you enter the museum, and organize your own museum visit in the form of a game. The museum also organizes special 90-minute guided tours for kids ages 5–10 and their families, and other tours just for kids, in which guides bring the collection to life through stories, games, and other activities. These are usually in French, but some guides can translate into English. Early

KID-FRIENDLY EATS The museum's **snack bar** is reasonably priced but can get extremely crowded between noon and 2. For organic take-out goodies, which you can eat in the shop—if you don't mind standing up—or munch discreetly on a park bench, try **Veggie** (38 rue de Verneuil, tel. 01–42–61–28–61). On Sunday mornings, an **organic food market** on the boulevard Raspail (métro: Sèvres-Babylone) has great picnic finds, including crêpes and hot U.S.-style muffins. For park benches, try the little square des Missions Étrangères off the rue du Bac or the square Boucicault near the Sèvres-Babylone métro; both have kids' play areas.

1 rue de la Légion d'Honneur,
7e. Métro: Assemblée Nationale

01-45-49-48-14 or
01-45-49-11-11
www.musee-orsay.fr

40 frs. adults 26 and
up (Su 30 frs.), 30 frs.
adults 18-25

T-W and F-Sa 10-6,
Th 10-9:45, Su 9-6

6 and up

silent films accompanied by a real piano player and concerts of turn-of-the-last-century music are also held at the museum for kids and their families.

In addition to lush Rodin sculpture, early movie posters, turn-of-the-century decorative art, and rare examples of early photography, the Musée d'Orsay displays works by some of France's greatest painters (Delacroix, Ingres). Favorites among many visitors are works by the aforementioned Impressionists and post-Impressionists, grouped on the museum's upper level. Along with paintings by Monet, Manet, Cézanne, Sisley, Pissarro, and Renoir, you find Van Gogh's *La chambre à Arles* (*The Room at Arles*) and Dégas's sculpture *Petite danseuse de quatorze ans* (*Little 14-Year-Old Dancer*), a model for budding ballerinas. Families planning a visit to Monet's house at Giverny, west of Paris (see Fondation Claude Monet), should definitely check out the artist's paintings displayed here, such as *Coquelicots* (*Poppies*), with its bright red blossoms on a lush green field.

HEY, KIDS! Want to feel like Mary Poppins, French-style? A glass floor lets you walk above the scale model of the Opéra neighborhood. The Opéra was *the* place to see and be seen in late-19th-century Paris, the period when most of the museum's works were created.

KEEP IN MIND If you arrive with a baby in a backpack or in a large stroller, you'll be asked to check it (the pack or stroller, not the baby) at the main desk. The museum lends folding strollers, though. For additional information about special family-oriented museum visits and activities, go to the Espace Jeunes (Youth Desk) on the museum's basement level or call 01-45-49-49-76. You can make reservations here (recommended) for guided tours, film screenings, and concerts.

MUSÉE DU LOUVRE

Just because the world's most famous museum is filled with priceless treasures that include Leonardo da Vinci's *Mona Lisa* and the *Venus de Milo* doesn't mean that kids will like it. The sheer size of this former palace makes it overwhelming for everyone, children especially. But that doesn't mean you should avoid it either. Your best strategy is to think of the Louvre as a long-term project, and plan to see only a small part of it each time you come. Pick up a free map at the museum's entrance and narrow your visit down to a few key areas. The useful "First Visit" brochure, in English, lists 50 top works of art and where to find them, although 50 is still too many for most kids.

The basic organization of the Louvre is actually simple: There are three main wings—Richelieu, Sully, and Denon. Of the three, Sully is probably your best bet with youngsters, because it's the wing with the mummies and other Egyptian artifacts. You can see sarcophagi, papyrus, and mummies of all sorts—people, cats, even fish—all wrapped up in their

KEEP IN MIND The museum's rue de Rivoli entrance usually has shorter lines. Come to the Louvre at night to see its stunning exterior artfully lit. The Louvre organizes excellent guided tours and workshops for kids (in French); call 01–40–20–53–17 for subjects and times.

HEY, KIDS! Hieroglyphics—the ancient Egyptian form of writing that uses pictures of objects to represent sounds and words—were a mystery until a French specialist on Egypt, Jean-Francois Champollion, figured them out in 1822. Five years later, he set up the Egyptian section of the Louvre. Check out the hieroglyphics on the *Palette au nom du roi Toutankhamon* (*Tablet in the Name of King Tutankhamen*) in the Civilisation Pharaonique (Civilization of the Pharaohs) room. It's a wooden tablet with sea-grass pens and ink holders from King Tut's day (around 1336–1327 BC). Imagine having to do your homework on something like this.

34–36 quai du Louvre and 99 rue de Rivoli, 1er. Métro: Louvre

01-40-20-53-17, 01-40-20-51-51 in English www.louvre.fr

 45 frs. adults 18 and up, after 3 and Su 26 frs., 1st Su of month free

M and Th–Su 9–6 (Richelieu Wing M to 9:45), W 9–9:45

7 and up

creepy bandages. Kids should like the incredibly realistic statue known as the *Seated Scribe,* which dates from the time of the Great Pyramids. You'll also find intricate Roman mosaics and Etruscan art, along with the Greek masterpieces the *Venus de Milo* and the *Winged Victory of Samothrace.*

The Denon Wing has paintings from the Italian Renaissance, and that means the *Mona Lisa,* which is sealed up under glass and always surrounded by worshipers. The only way for kids to get even a glimpse of the famous smile is to nudge their way through the crowd. The Denon Wing also includes the grandiose Galerie d'Apollon, which has a potential kid-pleaser, King Louis XV's crown; it's loaded down with jewels. Outside the Louvre, the I. M. Pei pyramid over the museum's main entrance is surrounded by fountains and a wide paved area where kids can run around.

KID-FRIENDLY EATS Under the museum in the chic Carrousel du Louvre shopping mall, the self-service **Universal Resto** (tel. 01–47–03–96–58) has fresh, reasonably priced food representing 12 different cuisines, from Lebanese to Tex-Mex. Trendy **Le Marly** (Palais du Louvre, 93 rue de Rivoli, tel. 01–49–26–06–60), a café overlooking the pyramid, isn't cheap by any means, but the view of the pyramid is one-of-a-kind. The most affordable option is to come here for afternoon coffee and pastry but not if you're in a hurry. See also Jardin des Tuileries and Jardins du Palais-Royal.

MUSÉE EN HERBE

If your kids say they hate museums, bring them here and prove them wrong. Paris's first museum just for children (*en herbe* means "young sprouts," as in kids) believes that the best way for youngsters to learn is to have fun and move around. Almost everything on display is meant to be touched, fiddled with, or laughed at, and children don't just walk through exhibits; they're given a treasure map that guides them on a quest. While small kids manipulate geometric objects in kid-friendly colors and sizes, bigger kids can create art on their own faces using the makeup that's always on hand.

Most permanent exhibits have to do with the arts—interactive displays illustrating perspective or color combinations, for example—but the innovative temporary exhibits (changing every six months or so) broaden the focus to include cultural topics, too. A recent exhibit took kids to Vietnam. They were given a set of questions and a map that led them through displays—a bustling city street, a typical house, a church, a food market—whose every inch they explored in search of answers. Through this game, children found

KEEP IN MIND Everything in this museum is in French, including the workshops, but many staff members speak English and everything is so hands-on that kids should be able to follow what's going on without much trouble. Workshops for kids 5–12 are held on Wednesdays and Saturdays at 3 and daily during long school vacations. Workshops for kids 3–5 are held on Wednesdays at 11. (Five-year-olds can choose either.) If you have kids who want to attend a workshop and others who don't, you can head off to the Jardin d'Acclimatation (see above) with one group while the others stay behind.

Bois de Boulogne. Métro: Porte-Maillot, Sablons

01–40–67–97–66

 17 frs. adults 18 and up, 14 frs. children 17 and under, free with ticket to Jardin d'Acclimatation, workshops 26 frs.

Su–F 10–6, Sa 2–6

3–12

out that most Vietnamese get around by bicycle, that they eat things not found in most of our supermarkets (unless your supermarket stocks dried fish and green papaya), and that Vietnamese art isn't what we usually study (perhaps portraits of Buddha instead of the *Mona Lisa*). Other inventive exhibits have taken a tour through a certain period of art history or encouraged youngsters to think about concepts like citizenship.

Along with the exhibits, the museum organizes special classes for kids of all ages in which they can do all sorts of things, from painting pictures and creating sculpture to putting together machines or putting on a show. First kids visit the special exhibition and then work in groups to create something based on what they've just seen. There's even a special baby-atelier workshop for kids 3–5. This place is museum as playtime, and it's been entertaining kids and teaching them things for 25 years.

HEY, KIDS! Do you have a birthday coming up? If so, bring along at least nine other kids and celebrate here. You get to play games with the museum's staff, explore the exhibits, make yourselves up, and eat some birthday cake. *Bonne anniversaire!*

KID-FRIENDLY EATS There are several dining possibilities in the Jardin d'Acclimatation, or if it's a nice day, have a picnic in the Bois de Boulogne (see above for both). One great spot is the Pré Catalan, in the center of the bois, which has kids' play equipment. If you have little kids in tow, you'll need a car or a bike to get here, however, as it's a long walk. Organic picnic goodies are available at **Les Nouveaux Robinsons** (14 rue des Graviers, Neuilly-sur-Seine, tel. 01–47–47–92–80), a supermarket/food co-op near the Pont-de-Neuilly métro stop.

MUSÉE GRÉVIN

Want to see Michael Jackson stand absolutely still? You can at this museum, because he's made out of wax, and so are a lot of other people you may or may not recognize. There's something slightly creepy about wax museums, with their eerily lifelike figures frozen in place as though under a witch's spell, but everyone usually has fun picking out people they know. And this wax museum has the added bonus of providing a very vivid tour through French history.

You'll see King François I meeting England's King Henry VIII in 1520, Louis XIV at a sumptuous party at the Château de Versailles, Marie-Antoinette in her cell in the Concièrgerie prison, Napoléon drinking tea with Josephine, and the French revolutionary leader Jean-Paul Marat murdered in his bathtub. (By the way, the bathtub here really is the one Marat died in; this is one tableau that's not for little kids.) There are also sections devoted to movie stars and to movers and shakers past and present, who are displayed in elaborately decorated tableaux complete with background sounds.

HEY, KIDS!
The world's most famous wax museum is Madame Tussaud's, which was opened in London in 1802 by a Frenchwoman. Madame Tussaud learned the tricks of her trade in Paris during the French revolution by making wax death masks of people who'd been guillotined. Creepy.

KID-FRIENDLY EATS
Homesick? Bite the bullet and head to the **Hard Rock Cafe** (14 bd. Montmartre, tel. 01–53–24–60–00). Where else can you chow down on a good burger, fajitas, or a "Love Me Tender" kids' meal (fried chicken fillets) while staring at Michael Jackson's pants? Jugglers, singers, and who knows what else may be on hand to entertain you. Earplugs are advised for parents. At **American Dream** (21 rue Daunou, tel. 01–42–60–99– 89), you can fill up on a burger or a U.S.-style brunch in a huge space filled with '50s movie memorabilia; kids are very welcome. See also Opéra Garnier.

10 bd. Montmartre, 9e. Métro: Richelieu-Drouot

 65 frs. ages 15 and up, 39 frs. children 6–14

 Apr–Aug, daily 1–7; Sept–Mar, daily 1–5:30; closed for renovation until June 2001

 01–47–70–85–05

7 and up

As for the contemporary personalities, fame is fleeting and so are these figures. They come and go depending on whether the people they represent are in the news. It's a formula that's attracted over 45 million visitors to the museum since it opened all the way back in 1882. Kids are bound to spot some familiar faces, like Madonna, who seems to be a permanent resident.

A high point for most youngsters is the Palais des Mirages; a sound-and-light extravaganza created for the 1900 world's fair, it's still wowing audiences. Best of all are the performances put on in the museum's in-house theater every afternoon. From top-class magic shows to mime acts, these shows are bound to be kid-pleasers. Besides, it's a relief to watch some real, live human beings after you've stared at all those wax people.

KEEP IN MIND Has the historical exhibit here whetted your appetite for more history? At the nearby Paris-Story movie theater (11 bis rue Scribe, tel. 01–42–66–62–06), you can see a 45-minute film on the 2,000-year-plus history of Paris in 12 different languages (thanks to headphones). A new version of the movie was inaugurated in October 2000. Kids should enjoy the images even if they can't follow everything in the narration. Shown every hour on the hour, it's a good bet for a rainy day. The cost is 50 frs. adults and 30 frs. children 6–18.

MUSÉE NATIONAL DES ARTS
D'AFRIQUE ET D'OCÉANIE

The various names this museum has had since it was built for an exhibition on France's colonies in 1931 reflect the country's evolving attitude toward the lands it once governed. First it was called the Museum of the Colonies, then it became the Museum of Overseas France, and now, as the National Museum of Arts from Africa and the South Pacific, it focuses on presenting the arts and other cultural artifacts of former French colonies that have achieved their independence. Whatever its name, the museum's exhibits of unusual art from Africa and elsewhere—and especially its giant aquarium, one of Europe's biggest— are bound to appeal to kids.

The museum's collection includes many very rare and beautiful pieces that show the talents of people throughout Africa and the French-speaking South Pacific and Caribbean. There are intricately carved statues and masks, stunning costumes worn by tribal chiefs on ceremonial occasions, more humble items meant for everyday use, and a huge assortment

HEY, KIDS! Know the differences between crocodiles and alligators? Crocs are longer (up to 20 feet), have a pointier snout, and have a gap in their upper jaw where the fourth tooth in their lower jaw fits. In the southern United States, alligators are much more common than crocodiles, though limited numbers of one species (*Crocodylus acutus*) are found in South Florida. (Neither species lives in France.) Crocodiles are the more aggressive creature, often attacking large animals, and people. They can live a century and have remained virtually unchanged for 200 million years, proof that, scary as they are, they're doing something right.

293 av. Daumesnil, 12e.
Métro: Porte Dorée

 01–44–74–85–00

 30 frs. adults 26 and up (Su 20 frs.), 20 frs. adults 18–25

 M and W–F 10–7:30, Sa–Su 10–6

 6 and up

of unusual musical instruments. Ask at the desk for a copy of the "Livret Parcours," a brochure (in French) that leads kids on a kind of treasure hunt through the collection.

The basement is the site of the museum's aquarium, parts of which date from 1931, when the museum opened. Not surprisingly, some of it looks a bit the worse for wear. Children won't notice that, though, once they see the turtle section; the flamboyantly colored, strange fish native to Africa and the South Pacific; and, most exciting of all, the big pit full of huge, ferocious, snapping crocodiles. Why a big aquarium in a museum devoted to African, Asian, and Caribbean arts? When the museum was opened, organizers thought it would be a good idea to display the native flora and fauna of the French colonies. Today, it's sure to be the part of the museum kids remember best.

KEEP IN MIND

On Wednesday afternoons, the museum organizes two-hour classes (in French) for kids 6 and older to teach them about the collection through games, stories, and other activities. Examples include decorating paper plates with aboriginal designs and making up faces Polynesian style.

KID-FRIENDLY EATS

There are several simple cafés in the Porte Dorée area, near the museum, where you can lunch on an omelet, a *croque monsieur* (grilled ham-and-cheese sandwich), and a *citron pressée* (fresh lemonade). There are also several food shops where you can get the makings for a picnic in the nearby Bois de Vincennes. **Les Zygomates** (7 rue de Capri, tel. 01–40–19–93–04) is a friendly bistro with inventive cooking and a reasonable fixed-price lunch menu on weekdays. If all else fails, there's a **McDonald's** (282 av. Daumesnil, tel. 01–46–28–00–51). See also Bois de Vincennes.

MUSÉE PICASSO

This museum devoted to the 20th century's most famous artist is housed in a palatial 17th-century mansion in the heart of the Marais district. A real effort has been made to get kids enthusiastic about the art displayed here through free guided art-appreciation tours (in French). On the tours, kids take a good look at an artwork, ask questions about it, and discuss it with a very competent staff member. But even if your children can't participate in these tours, they should enjoy the art in the collection. Among the thousands of works by Picasso are 200 paintings, sculptures, and ceramics and over 3,000 drawings and prints. The museum also displays Picasso's personal art collection, which includes works by Derain, Cézanne, Modigliani, Renoir, Rousseau, Braque, and other 20th-century greats whom he admired.

HEY, KIDS!

Pablo Picasso was born in Malaga, Spain, where his great artistic talent was recognized very early. The first public showing of his works was held when he was just 16. After a visit to Paris three years later, he moved to France and stayed.

Children often seem to respond better to contemporary art than adults do. They accept it on its own terms, and, in the case of Picasso, respond to his playfulness. Kids of all

KID-FRIENDLY EATS **Fromagers de France** (39 rue de Bretagne, tel. 01–42–78–52–61) is a superb cheese store; try a French kids' favorite, nutty *cantal*. **Brocco** (180 rue du Temple, tel. 01–42–72–19–81) is a pastry shop and tearoom with gooey pastries and an elaborately painted 1889 ceiling. **Finkelsztajn** (27 rue des Rosiers, tel. 01– 42–72–78–91) is a bakery selling high-quality take-out snacks, including bagels, poppy-seed pastries, indecently rich cheesecake, and decadent eggplant dip. See also Centre National d'Art et de Culture Georges Pompidou, Musée de la Curiosité et de la Magie, and Place des Vosges and the Marais.

Hôtel Salé, 5 rue de Thorigny, 3e. Métro: Chemin Vert

 30 frs. adults 26 and up, 28 frs. adults 18–25

 W and F–M 9:30–5:30, Th 9:30–8

01–42–71–25–21
www.oda.fr/aa/musee-picasso

10 and up

ages wander through the galleries here, picking out works they like. Some prefer the "pink period," others the "blue period," but most are impressed by the huge *Têtes monumentales* (*Monumental Heads*) in the sculpture gallery. After viewing the collection, take a break in the museum's lovely garden or pick out an art poster in the gift shop.

In case your children ask, the building's name, Hôtel Salé, means "salted townhouse," which came from the fact that its original owner, Aubert de Fontenay, made his fortune by being the sole collector of a French tax on salt. There's a certain poetic justice in this, because after Picasso's death his heirs gave his private collection to the French government in lieu of paying inheritance taxes, and the government in turn created this museum to house the collection. Any way you look at it, it's a museum that taxes built.

KEEP IN MIND Nearby, another small museum in a mansion, the Musée Carnavalet (23 rue de Sevigné, tel. 01–42–72–21–13), is dedicated to the history of Paris (closed Monday). Kids like the fantastically detailed scale models of some of the city's houses and neighborhoods as they were in the past, and a model of a guillotine carved out of bone by French prisoners of war. The museum offers lots of organized activities for children, including the Paris en Jeux class, which takes children on a tour of the Marais district in the form of a game (in French).

MUSÉE RODIN

The elegant 18th-century Hôtel Biron, Rodin's home for the last decade of his life, contains many of the sculptor's best-known works, including *Les bourgeois de Calais* (*The Burghers of Calais*) and *Le penseur* (*The Thinker*). Several of the sculptures are displayed in the 5-plus-acre garden surrounding the house, which has beautifully planted flower beds, trees, a sandbox, and lots of benches. You usually find Parisian parents reading quietly here, while their babies doze and their older kids run around and play. Rodin's massive yet fluid and lifelike sculptures form a calming background in this peaceful scene.

If you thought of Rodin as a struggling artist working in a tiny garret, think again; his mansion is an elegant white stone building with tall windows overlooking the garden. Within, you find some of Rodin's smaller sculptures as well as drawings and art from his personal collection—including works by Monet, Van Gogh, Camille Claudel, and other artists Rodin knew—all displayed in the mansion's large, high-ceilinged rooms.

KID-FRIENDLY EATS The Rodin museum's reasonably priced in-house **café** has tables in the garden (open April–September). Two nearby restaurants known for their classic cuisine and low prices are **Au Pied de Fouet** (45 rue de Babylone, tel. 01–47–05–12–27) and **Chez Germaine** (30 rue Pierre-Leroux, tel. 01–42–73–28–34). **Than** (42 rue des Sts-Pères, tel. 01–45–48–36–97) has good *nem* (Vietnamese egg rolls) and other Vietnamese specialties at bargain prices. **Le Coffee Saint-German** (5 rue Perronet, tel. 01–40–49–08–08) is *the* place for burgers, brownies, and a yummy U.S.-style weekend brunch.

Although younger kids usually prefer the museum's garden (where they can run around) to its interior (where they need to be sedate and well behaved), older kids enjoy seeing the varied works of art and maybe even trying a little sculpting themselves. Every Wednesday afternoon from 2:30 to 4:30 and several times a week during school holidays, the museum organizes art classes for kids: one session for children 6–10, another for youths 11–15. (While your kids are busy in their classes, you can take a guided tour of the museum's collection.) Children are encouraged to have a close encounter with one of the museum's artworks and then to try their hands at sculpting in wax, clay, or plaster along a particular theme. They can even take their finished piece with them. (Bring a shoe box to take it home safely as well as an apron or smock to protect clothes.) Though sessions are in French, even non-French-speakers should be able to enjoy these popular hands-on lessons, but reserve well in advance.

KEEP IN MIND
Sample kids' workshop themes have included faces and feelings, hands that speak, dance and sculpture, and the creation of city monuments. This small museum is definitely committed to helping kids perceive art in new ways. It's no wonder Parisian parents love bringing their kids here.

HEY, KIDS! The great sculptor Rodin trained to be a mason and then, after visiting a few museums, got interested in sculpture. After a trip to Italy in 1875 he began an early work, *L'Age de bronze (The Bronze Age)*, displayed in the museum here. That's where his artistic career could have ground to a halt, because the sculpture cost him a great deal of time and money, and people attacked it because they thought it was too realistic. Rodin had the last word, though. His natural, realistic style eventually caught on, and he became one of the world's most famous artists.

MUSÉE VIVANT DU CHEVAL

Once upon a time (in 1719), a French prince, Louis-Henri de Bourbon, Prince de Condé, had a vision: When he died, he would be reborn—as a horse. The prince, who was very rich, decided to build a horse château worthy of a princely horse. He asked the most famous architect of the time to create Les Grandes Écuries (The Great Stables) facing his own fabulous Château de Chantilly, in the middle of a huge forest north of Paris. The prince died, perhaps becoming one of the 300 or so horses that lived in Les Grandes Écuries throughout the 18th century. Here they were visited by the likes of King Louis XV.

Today, Les Grandes Écuries is still the home of pampered horses, as well as of the Musée Vivant du Cheval (Living Museum of the Horse), which welcomes around 200,000 visitors a year. Kids like seeing the stable complex, which looks from the outside like an elegant château. Inside it's filled with around 40 well-groomed horses, swishing their tails in their luxurious boxes in a huge hall with a vaulted stone ceiling. The museum has more than

KID-FRIENDLY EATS In the museum, **Le Carrousel Gourmand** (weekends only in winter) has a children's menu. **Touche Nature** (22 rue de Connétable, tel. 03–44–57–02–25), a family-friendly bistro, serves organic foods. *Crème Chantilly* (whipped cream) tops cookies at stands around town in summer.

KEEP IN MIND Equestrian shows are given several times in December and on the first weekend of the month the rest of the year (8:30 PM Saturday for the popular "Cheval et Gospel" show, featuring gospel singers, and 3:15 PM Sunday for "Le Cheval à Travers les Peintres," in which horses appear in scenes evoking famous paintings). Reservations are advised (80–150 frs. ages 13 and up, 70–120 frs. children 4–12). The Château de Chantilly contains the Musée du Condé (tel. 03–44–62–62–62), which has an excellent art collection, but it's not oriented to kids at all.

30 exhibit rooms with all sorts of objects relating to horses over the ages.

The main attractions, however, are the equestrian shows performed regularly in the museum's elegant *manège* (ring). Shows are based on an easy-to-follow story or theme. You sit very near the beautiful horses, who, along with their riders, wear elaborate costumes. An orchestra plays in the background. Every year in December, special Christmas shows for kids are performed, in which Santa (riding a horse or donkey) has a lot of trouble delivering his gifts. He's helped by various characters, all of whom perform spectacular acts on horseback. The elegant park that surrounds the château and stables was designed by the great Le Nôtre. Kids can run off energy as parents admire the park's fountains and flowers, and in summer the whole family can take a ride on the Aérophile hot-air balloon, which is tethered to the ground but rises almost 150 meters (500 feet) above the park.

TRANSPORTATION Several trains per day run from the Gare du Nord to Chantilly–Les Gouviers. The trip takes 30 minutes, but you will have about a 20-minute walk from the train station in Chantilly to the museum. Taxis are another option from the station, but you might have to wait in a long line. If you go by car from Paris, take the A1 highway from the Porte de la Chapelle, on the northern edge of Paris, and head north to the Survilliers-Chantilly exit. Signs in the center of Chantilly point you to the Musée Vivant du Cheval.

MUSÉUM NATIONAL D'HISTOIRE NATURELLE

France's natural-history museum is actually several museums in the Jardin des Plantes, each focusing on a different aspect of natural history. The showcase collection is the state-of-the-art Grande Galerie de l'Évolution (Grand Gallery of Evolution).

Using the latest bells and whistles, such as interactive touch screens and games, this gallery makes natural history exciting and fun. Kids are immediately attracted to the life-size models of African animals marching through the main hall, led by an elephant and towered over by a giraffe. Displays showing animal habitats come with light shows and sounds to bring the habitats alive. In the gallery's upper level, models of extinct creatures include the dodo, and there's a skeleton of a blue whale suspended from the ceiling, too. Everything is housed in a huge, modern, perfectly lit space with plenty of room to move.

If your taste runs to mysterious specimens amassed by intrepid French naturalists, you'll be fascinated by the quirky Galerie de Paléontologie et d'Anatomie Comparée (Paleontology

HEY, KIDS! Whales are full of surprises. They look like fish, but they're not. They're mammals that suckle their young the way humans do. The blue whale whose skeleton hangs over your head in the evolution gallery is the biggest mammal the world has ever known. And as for the narwhal, it has a 6-foot-long, coiled ivory tusk, which makes it look like a unicorn in arctic waters. Whales have been hunted for centuries for their meat, their oil, their bones, and the ivory tusk of the narwhal.

36 rue Geoffroy-St-Hilaire, 5e. Métro: Jussieu, Austerlitz

01-40-79-30-00
www.mnhn.fr

Evolution gallery 40 frs. ages 16 and up, 30 frs. children 5–15 (55 frs. and 40 frs. including temporary exhibits); other galleries 30 frs. ages 16 and up, 20 frs. children

M and W–Su 10–6, Th 10–10

6 and up

and Comparative Anatomy Gallery). When you walk in, you might want to walk right back out again, because an enormous mass of skeletons—hippos, giraffes, elephants—seems to be marching straight at you, along with a man wearing a fig leaf but no skin (so you can see his skeleton, too). There's even a room with skeletons of a dinosaur and mammoth. This museum also has a collection of creepy oddities, many collected by 19th-century naturalists, including pickled monkeys, pickled human brains, a pickled Cyclops cat (no kidding), and skeletons of Siamese twins, all proving that Mother Nature is not always kind.

The Galerie de Minéralogie (Mineralogy Gallery) has a stunning collection of gemstones and rocks; the Galerie de Paléobotanique (Paleobotany Gallery) features fossils and petrified wood, including a 33-million-year-old petrified fern; and the Galerie d'Entomologie (Entomology Gallery) displays 1,500 rare bug specimens. It's an amazing collection of things natural.

KEEP IN MIND
To beat the crowds in the popular Grande Galerie d'Évolution, avoid a weekend visit. Some of the pickled items in the Galerie de Paléobotanique et d'Anatomie Comparée may be too macabre for very young children (or their parents).

KID-FRIENDLY EATS Have lunch with a giraffe, an elephant, and skeletons in the Grande Galerie d'Évolution's spacious, ultramodern **cafeteria,** overlooking the main gallery. You'll also find **snack stands** in the Jardin des Plantes. **Mavrommatis** (47 rue Censier, tel. 01–45–35–96–50) has delicious Greek takeout goodies for a park-bench picnic. **L'Arrivé** (14 bd. de l'Hopital, tel. 01–43–31–18–72) is a bustling restaurant featuring family- style cooking near the Gare d'Austerlitz. See also Jardin des Plantes and Jardin de Sculpture en Pleine Air.

NATURE ET DÉCOUVERTES

Want to learn how to identify trees by touch or go bird-watching in a Paris park with a guide? You and your family can do just these things thanks to Nature et Découvertes (Nature and Discovery), a national chain of stores that French kids and parents love. All the stores organize free workshops and almost-free family outings designed to teach people about environmental issues in a fun way.

The Carrousel du Louvre store gives one-hour kids' workshops every Wednesday. Children spend an hour with an instructor doing creative activities with specific themes; learning to identify different types of leaves and making plaster casts of animal tracks are just some of the many possibilities. Classes are given in French, but most instructors speak English and can provide some translation help. If you have younger kids in tow, you and they can have fun looking at the hundreds of Earth-friendly items in the store while older siblings

KID-FRIENDLY EATS The Carrousel du Louvre's **Universal Resto** (tel. 01–47–03–96–58) contains many food outlets representing cuisines from around the world; there's bound to be something to please everyone in your group. For above-ground choices, see Musée du Louvre and Jardins du Palais-Royal.

KEEP IN MIND Pick up the "Programme des Animations Pédagogiques" brochure, which lists upcoming workshops and outings. You're supposed to reserve (and pay) in advance for the longer outings (in the store, by phone, or on the Internet), and it's a good idea to reserve for the workshops, since space is limited. For outings, you provide your own transportation. Other Paris Nature et Découvertes locations are in the Forum des Halles (105 rue Rambuteau, 1er, tel. 01–40–28–42–16), an underground mall; in the Palais de la Découverte (see below); and at 61 rue de Passy, 16e, tel. 01–42–30–53–87.

Carrousel du Louvre mall, 99 rue de Rivoli, 1er. Métro: Louvre

 01–47–03–47–43 www.natureetdecouvertes.com

Workshops free; outings 30 frs. ages 12 and up, some outings extra

Store daily 10–8, workshops W varying hrs

 Store: all ages; workshops and outings: 8 and up

are in the workshop. The store has a wide range of unusual toys (some of which are always available for kids to try out), gadgets, books, CDs, and outdoor gear, and there's always a kid-oriented video being screened.

Family outings (also for anyone 8 and over) are for members of the Nature et Découvertes Club, which you can join for free at any of the stores, though a 50-fr. membership gives you some added perks. These outings take place outside the store and last about 90 minutes, sometimes longer. You and a small group led by a well-informed guide might go bird-watching or check out plant and animal life in a Paris-area forest. The outings provide the whole family with a great introduction to Paris's environmental issues, not to mention an introduction to French people with similar interests.

HEY, KIDS! Some items in the Nature et Découvertes stores have fastenings made from Velcro. Did you know that Velcro is a high-tech version of burrs, those prickly things that hang on your clothes when you're playing in a field? Velcro was created by Georges de Mestral, an inventor from the French-speaking part of Switzerland, who came up with the idea after studying how burrs attach themselves to things. He noticed that burrs are covered with hundreds of tiny hooks. The word "Velcro" comes from two French words: *velours* (velvet) and *crochet* (hook).

OPÉRA GARNIER

If you want your children to see an architectural landmark that sums up everything that was Paris in the mid-19th century, the Opéra Garnier is the place to go. Dripping with gilt and covered with every possible kind of adornment, from charging horses to the heads of composers, the Opéra Garnier was considered the height of sophistication in the days when Paris was recognized as the world's cultural capital.

The best way to introduce kids to the Opéra Garnier is to bring them to a performance here. Works that appeal to younger audiences (such as *The Nutcracker* or *The Magic Flute*) are programmed all year long and are performed by some of the world's top musicians and dancers. Even the most blasé kids can't help but be impressed by all the red plush, gilt, and general overblown elegance of the opera house's interior, especially when the orchestra starts tuning up and the curtain starts to rise on what's billed as the world's biggest stage.

KID-FRIENDLY EATS If you have teens dying to shop for the latest fashions, visit the nearby Printemps and Galeries Lafayette department stores on the boulevard Haussmann and have lunch afterwards in **Flo-Printemps** (64 bd. Haussmann, tel. 01–42–82–58–81), a classy brasserie on the 6th floor of the Printemps de la Mode building. Historic **Café de la Paix** (5 pl. de l'Opéra, tel. 01–40–07–30–10) is just barely affordable for afternoon tea. Come to friendly **Kildare Irish Pub** (6 bis rue Quatre-Septembre, tel. 01–47–03–91–91) for Irish stew and gooey desserts. See also Musée Grévin.

8 rue Scribe, 9e. Métro: Opéra

01-40-01-19-88 or 08-36-69-78-78 www.opera-de-paris.com

 30 frs. ages 16 and up, 20 frs. youths 10–15; tours 60 frs. ages 16 and up, 45 frs. youths, 25 frs. children 9 and under

Daily 10–5; English tour daily at 3

 6 and up

Even if an opera performance doesn't fit into your agenda, you can take a guided tour of the Opéra Garnier (tours in English are available) or stroll around on your own to check out the monumental marble staircase, the 11,000-square-meter (118,000-square-foot) stage, and the main auditorium's fanciful ceiling, painted by Marc Chagall in 1964. To make all this more accessible for kids, the Opéra Garnier organizes innovative 90-minute *visites-ateliers jeune publique* (tour-workshops for children) on Wednesdays (in French). The Phantom of the Opera leads kids 4–6 around and tells them stories about all the things that have happened here, while kids 7–12 work with artists to draw elements of the decor or create their own opera costumes out of cloth. These classes show kids that opera isn't just for adults; it's for them, too.

HEY, KIDS! Check out the enormous crystal chandelier in the Opéra Garnier's red-and-gold auditorium. It used to hold hundreds of candles, but now it's electric. You wouldn't want it to fall on your head: It weighs eight tons. The question is, how did they light all those candles?

KEEP IN MIND The auditorium is closed to visitors during rehearsals; ask when you buy your ticket whether it will be open the day you visit. Reserve at least two weeks in advance for the kids' tour-workshops (tel. 01-40-01-22-63). Special *spectacles jeune publique* (performances for kids 5–13) are organized here and at the Opéra de la Bastille (100 frs. ages 14 and up, 35 frs. children 13 and under). Reserve well in advance.

OYA, JEUX À JOUER

Does your family love to play cards and board games? If so, come to this games store and game-playing center, where you can find great new games that you'd probably never come across otherwise, since most aren't distributed in the United States. Oya has a collection of hundreds of games produced by a group of German companies that uses the innovative store–playing center combo to make their games more interesting and accessible to the public. Instead of taking potluck and buying a game off the shelf, you get to test it first in a "try before you buy" session. And the best part is, you don't ever have to buy anything. You can come just to play with any of the games, designed for different age groups and numbers of players. This is a good spot to take a break on a rainy day.

Start by choosing a table (the center has several tables and can handle up to 60 game-players at a time), and ask the very friendly, English-speaking staff for suggestions of

KEEP IN MIND When it comes to asking staff for a game suggestion, be specific. Let the person know the types of games your family likes and how much experience you have in playing them. That way you're more likely to get a game that's right for you.

HEY, KIDS! People have played board games for thousands of years. The oldest known game is Senet, a forerunner of backgammon played in Egypt 4,000 years ago. It was very popular—sort of the Nintendo of the pharaohs. In fact, Senet boards have been found carved on many ancient Egyptian monuments, including tombs (for something to do when the afterlife got boring?). The world's most-played board games today are said to be checkers, Go, backgammon, chess, and Mancala (played by millions of people in Africa and the Middle East). Maybe you'll find the next classic here at Oya.

25 rue de la Reine Blanche, 13e.
Métro: Gobelins

01–47–07–59–59

 Play: 1st game 30 frs., 2nd game 15 frs.; play and snack: 35 frs.

T–Su 2–12

6 and up

appropriate games. A staff member will bring you a game to try out and, since the instructions that come with the games are in German and French, can explain the rules to you in English, speaking slowly enough for you to write them down. Staff are also ready to help if you have questions while playing. If you want to try a second game, there's a smaller extra charge.

One sample on hand is Schotten-Totten, a deceptively simple card game for two players ages 8 and up. (Its name in English is Highlander.) The rules are easy to grasp, but the game itself calls for lots of strategy and bluffing, certain to please kids, especially since they can often beat their parents. Other options might be geared to larger groups or to older kids and adults. Of course, you are always welcome to buy a game to take home; prices range from around 70 frs. up to 250 frs. (very reasonable for Paris).

KID-FRIENDLY EATS Oya has a **snack bar,** where you can get ice cream, candy bars, and sodas or coffee. **Le Jardin des Pâtes** (33 bd. Arago, tel. 01–45–35–93–67) features pasta dishes made with organic ingredients. **Le Timri** (41 rue Vandrezanne, tel. 01–45–65–23–87) has couscous and grilled meats with fries. See also Médaillons d'Arago, Muséum National d'Histoire Naturelle, and the Catacombes.

PALAIS DE CHAILLOT

18

The grandiose Palais de Chaillot, created for the 1937 Paris world's fair, is surrounded by the terraced Jardins de Trocadéro park and offers great views of the Tour Eiffel across the river. Chaillot contains two museums kids enjoy: the Musée de l'Homme (Museum of Mankind) and the Musée de la Marine (Naval History Museum).

The Musée de l'Homme traces human history through exhibits on arts, crafts, and rituals. The huge space devoted to prehistoric peoples houses an exhibit on the magnificent animal drawings made by France's own cave-dwellers. The section on crafts and rituals includes musical instruments made by people with little means but a lot of imagination. In the À la Rencontre des Amériques (Discovery of America) exhibition, check out the magnificent red porphyry statue of Quetzalcoatl (the plumed serpent), created in Mexico in the 15th century. Kids should especially enjoy the Tous Parents, Tous Differents (All the Same Family, All Different) section, where an interactive display lets them create faces from a database of 118 pairs of eyes, 66 noses, 81 mouths, and 185 hairlines.

KEEP IN MIND If your smaller children have an attack of museum overload, treat them to a ride on one of Paris's oldest and most beautiful merry-go-rounds, set up in the Trocadéro gardens just below the Palais de Chaillot. And if you have any skateboarders or rollerbladers in your crowd, bring them here to zoom along with Paris's best skaters and boarders, who strut their stuff on the Trocadéro's terraces. If you happen to be in Paris on July 14, Bastille Day, the Palais de Chaillot is the perfect place to watch the magnificent fireworks display held at the Tour Eiffel.

17 pl. du Trocadéro, 16e. Métro: Trocadéro

01-44-05-72-72
www.mnhn.fr

Musée de l'Homme: 30 frs. adults 19 and up, 20 frs. youths 12–18, 10 frs. children 11 and under; Musée de la Marine: 38 frs. adults 26 and up, 25 frs. ages 8–25

W–M 9:45–5:15

6 and up

The Musée de la Marine is the world's second-oldest naval-history museum after St. Petersburg's and demonstrates France's long history as a sailing nation. Here kids should like the gilded figures that once adorned *La Réale,* a ship in Louis XIV's navy, as well as a collection of sextants and other nautical instruments from the past. Budding sailors have a great time identifying the models of various vessels and can watch the museum's craftspeople creating and repairing other models.

Both the Musée de l'Homme and the Musée de la Marine regularly organize children's crafts workshops, and the Musée de l'Homme regularly screens documentary films suitable for kids. The Palais de Chaillot also contains the Musée des Monuments Français (Museum of French Monuments), closed for renovation until 2003.

HEY, KIDS! Sailors used the antique sextants in the Musée de la Marine (though they weren't antiques yet) to calculate latitude by measuring the angle formed by a heavenly body (like a star), the ship, and the horizon. You can learn how to do it at the museum.

KID-FRIENDLY EATS **Le Totem** (tel. 01–47–27–28–29), a café in the Musée de l'Homme, serves light lunches, afternoon pastry, and classic French cuisine in the evening. Kids like the totem poles and the great Tour Eiffel views. **La Butte Chaillot** (110 bis av. Kléber, tel. 01–47–27–88–88), a chic bistro run by famous chef Guy Savoy, has a kids' menu at lunch on weekends and fixed-price menus for parents. So the whole family can have a gourmet feast at a reasonable (though not cheap) price. Kids can play a "guess this scent" game and receive a diploma signed by the chef. Reservations are advised.

PALAIS DE LA DÉCOUVERTE

The sprawling Palais de la Découverte (Palace of Discovery) opened in the 1930s and was pretty stodgy until a recent extensive remodeling. Now hands-on displays illustrating scientific principles are bound to please curious kids. One drawback: All the explanatory texts, all the video clips, and all the gadget labels are in French. Still, even if you can't understand the language, it's fun to push buttons, make sounds, and learn how to handle various devices by watching French kids play with them. And there will be a lot of French kids here no matter when you visit, because Paris schools routinely come here on field trips.

One exhibit allows you to make lightning, another to whirl the planets around the sun, another to view the effects of static electricity on your own hair, and still another to make a visual display of sounds using an oscilloscope. The École de Rats (Rats' School) is a

KEEP IN MIND The Palais de la Découverte organizes classes for kids (in French) and some of Paris's most exciting special exhibitions, always designed with kids in mind. Check local events listings for details on what's happening when you visit.

KID-FRIENDLY EATS Affordable eateries in this high-priced neighborhood include three child-friendly chains: **Hippopotamus** (42 av. de Champs-Élysées, tel. 01–53–83–94–50), **Bistro Romain** (26 av. de Champs-Élysées, tel. 01–43–59–93–31), and **McDonald's** (140 av. de Champs-Élysées, tel. 01–53–77–21–00). Kids love **Planet Hollywood** (78 av. de Champs-Élysées, tel. 01– 53–83–78–27) for its burgers, barbecue, hot-fudge sundaes, coloring books, and wild movie-land decor. The **Chicago Pizza Pie Factory** (5 rue de Berri, tel. 01–45–62–50–23) has deep-dish pizza and a special kids-only lunch (weekends 1–2) at the bar, complete with clowns and magicians.

Av. Franklin-Roosevelt, 8e. Métro:
Franklin Roosevelt

 01–40–74–81–82
www.palais-decouverte.fr

 30 frs. adults 18 and up
plus 15 frs. per additional
person 6 and up; planetarium 15 frs. ages 6 and up

 T–Sa 9:30–6

3 and up

fascinating demonstration of how animals learn. Acoustics, electromagnetic fields, spectrography, genetics, the workings of a color television, and biochemistry are among the subjects made accessible—and fun—by the museum's creative exhibits.

The planetarium, which has a 15-meter-high (50-foot) ceiling and seats 200, is worth a visit for its celestial show illustrating the movements of stars and planets. Even kids who don't understand the accompanying French narration can pick out familiar constellations and watch the solar system in action. The museum's popular gallery dedicated to space exploration, sure to please science-fiction-lovers, displays a gift to the museum from the United States: a fragment of moon rock brought back by the *Apollo 11* crew in 1969. Like the museum, it's the essence of discovery.

HEY, KIDS! One thing you'll learn if you visit the planetarium is that the names of constellations can be very different in French and English. For example, in France, the Big Dipper and the Little Dipper are called La Grande Ourse and La Petite Ourse, meaning the Great Bear and the Little Bear (from their Latin names: Ursa Major and Ursa Minor). On the other hand, Orion, the legendary Greek hunter and giant who found his way to the heavens, is called Orion in both languages.

PARC ANDRÉ CITROËN

This vast park covering 14 hectares (about 35 acres) on the banks of the Seine has come full circle. In the early 19th century, there was a village here, named Javel, surrounded by a big, grassy pasture known for its wildflowers. The street near the park that's now called rue des Cévennes used to be called rue des Marguerites (Daisy Street). As Paris became more and more industrialized, a big bleach factory was built on part of the pasture (bleach in France is still called *eau de Javel*), and car-maker André Citroën built a gigantic automobile assembly plant on what was left of the open space. Both factories were eventually torn down to make way for this park, and today it offers many attractions for kids.

Now that the open space has been restored, kids can run on the grass and snoop in a series of gardens with different themes: the Jardin Blanc (White Garden), which has all white flowers; the Jardin Noir (Black Garden), containing all dark flowers; the Jardin des

KEEP IN MIND Be prepared for some begging from your children. The park's Fortis Balloon (tel. 01–44–26– 20–00) is billed as the world's biggest hot-air balloon. It's tethered to the ground, so it doesn't go anywhere except up and down, but the ride is still exciting, taking you over 135 meters (450 feet) above the park. Rides are given daily every 15 minutes from 9:30 to dusk. Note that if you visit this park on a hot summer day, take a tip from Parisian parents and come equipped with bathing suits. Your kids are inevitably going to get soaked to the skin playing in the fountains; that's what's fun about this place.

Bordered by quai André Citroën, rue St-Charles, rue Balard, 15e. Métro: Javel

 Free

 June–Aug, Su–T 8:30–8:30, W–Sa 8:30 AM–9:30 PM; Sept–May, Su–T 8:30–6:30, W–Sa 8:30–7

01–45–57–13–35

All ages

Métamorphoses, with plants that are supposed to evoke the colors of seven metals (heavy metal goes green?); the Jardin des Roches (Rock Garden), which is meant for kids to climb on; and, in a gesture to the area's past, a garden dedicated to wildflowers. There's also a labyrinth that kids love to lose you in, as well as two greenhouses.

This park's biggest attraction for kids, though, is without a doubt the fountains near the Jardin Noir. On computer-controlled timers, they gush forth in unpredictable ways. Best of all, children are allowed to run around in them. This is an ideal spot to bring your kids on a hot summer day. All year long, though, they can work off steam on the climbing equipment, swings, and slides in the play area next to the Jardin Blanc.

HEY, KIDS! It's hard to believe today, but archaeologists have discovered fossil evidence that proves that the rue St-Charles, one of the busy streets that runs along the edge of this park, crosses a trail used thousands of years ago by woolly mammoths and rhinoceroses.

KID-FRIENDLY EATS Durand Dupont Drugstore (14 rue Cauchy, tel. 01–45–54–43–43) isn't a drugstore at all but a spacious restaurant popular for Sunday brunch. **Al Wady** (153 rue de Lourmel, tel. 01–45–58– 57–18) is one of Paris's best Lebanese restaurants; order a big plate of *mezze* (appetizers) to please everyone. **Au Cochon Rose** (137 rue St-Charles, tel. 01–45–78–03–68) has picnic goodies. **Pâtisserie Lecoq** (120 rue St-Charles, tel. 01–45–77–72– 56) offers temptations like the Arcachon, filled with chocolate mousse. See also Aquaboulevard.

PARC ASTÉRIX

The Parc Astérix, in a huge forest north of Paris, is the French equivalent of Disneyland, with Mickey and crew replaced by Astérix and his band of jovial Gauls (from a hugely popular and oft-translated comic-book series). Throughout the park, actors stage performances that almost bring French history to life—though the focus is on fun rather than historical accuracy—and leave kids with a vivid impression of a bunch of rambunctious Gauls making life miserable for the invading Romans. Action-loving kids find outstanding rides they won't soon forget.

The park is divided into six themed areas: the village of the Gauls, ancient Rome, ancient Greece, the Middle Ages, the 17th century, and modern times. In the first two, actors perform scenes starring the comic-strip characters every French kid knows: little, clever Astérix (the Gauls' hero); powerful, fat, gluttonous Obélix (whose job is hauling *menhirs,* huge stones the Gauls considered magic) and his dog Idée-Fixe; Panoramix, the Gauls' clever Druid; Assurancetourix, the local (bad) poet; and Abraracourcix, the Gauls' leader, fearless

KID-FRIENDLY EATS The park is filled with 40 different snack bars and restaurants, such as **Fastfoodus** and **Selfservix** (you get the idea). At the **Cirque** (circus) eatery, you can sample Obélix's favorite: wild boar (in pâté). There are several picnic areas, too.

TRANSPORTATION By car, take the A1 highway north from Paris to the Parc Astérix exit. The trip is around 35 kilometers (22 miles) and takes about 45 minutes, depending on traffic. By rail, take the RER commuter train, line B, to Charles–de–Gaulle airport, terminal 1, from which you can take a Courriers Ile–de–France bus to the park entrance. Signs in the airport indicate where the bus stop is. Buses leave every 30 minutes. A combination Parc Astérix–transportation pass (219 frs. ages 12 and up, 149 frs. children), sold at most métro and RER stations, covers the train, bus, and park admission.

Near the village of Plailly

03-36-68-30-10
www.parcasterix.com

  175 frs. ages 12 and up,
125 frs. children 3–11

 Apr–Sept, M–F 10–7, Sa–Su 9:30–8;
Oct, W and Sa–Su 10–7

3 and up

except when he thinks the sky is going to fall on his head. Stroll through the 17th century, and you're bound to see d'Artagnan and the other Musketeers in a wild sword fight.

Rides suit all tastes and ages, from an old-fashioned merry-go-round to one of Europe's tallest, scariest roller coasters, the Tonnerre de Zeus (Zeus's Thunder). Other top picks are the Goudurix, a coaster that does figure eights, and a walk through the Forêt des Druides (Druids' Forest), where stones talk, giant trees turn out to be super-high slides, and Druids do creepy experiments with giant mushrooms. Youngsters can join a parade led by Astérix and his men or ride the Serpentin, a low-key roller coaster. The whole family should like the performing dolphins at the Théâtre de Poséidon and the magic shows at the Théâtre de Panoramix. On hot summer days, ride the Menhir Express (with a 13-meter/43-foot swoop) or the less-scary Descente du Styx (Descent of the River Styx) roller coasters; you're guaranteed to get drenched.

HEY, KIDS! Obélix—the one with the big stomach—is so strong that his job is hauling around huge stones that weigh at least a ton. How did he get so powerful? When Obélix was a little boy, the Druid Panoramix concocted a magic potion to make the Gauls strong before a fight with the Romans, and Obélix—who never says no to anything to eat or drink—drank too much of it. Now Panoramix won't let him have any more potion, so he has to be satisfied with his next-favorite treat: roasted wild boar.

PARC DE LA VILLETTE

This huge park, which replaced decaying warehouses and slaughterhouses, is a park for the new century. There are few formal flower gardens here and few lawns you can't walk on. Instead, you find huge expanses of grass for running, curving sidewalks (good for rollerblading), bike trails, little bridges crossing a canal, and wonderful gardens and play areas designed to spark kids' imaginations.

The most exciting garden for most children is the Jardin de Dragon (Dragon Garden), which contains an enormous dragon-shape climbing structure that you can descend via stairs or a long, long, long curving slide. In the Jardin des Miroirs (Garden of Mirrors), mirrors reflect magically into a densely planted band of trees. The Jardin des Frayeurs Enfantines (Garden of Things that Scare Kids) won't scare kids at all, although its strange deep-jungle noises are fun to hear in the middle of such a big city. The Jardin des Vents et des Dunes (Garden of Wind and Dunes) has a series of weird humps and mounds that children are supposed to climb on while trying to keep their balance, along with air mattresses, kites, big pieces

KEEP IN MIND ZaziVillette (tel. 01–40–03–75–47) is a series of family-oriented performances either in the open air (Echaptout, usually free) or in the Grande Halle theater (Croq'Tout, 60 frs. for one adult and one child). In the latter, families go behind the scenes during and after the show. The Festival du Cinema de Plein Air (tel. 01–40–03–76–92) is a series of free open-air movies shown on a giant screen in the park (July–August, around 10 PM). You can rent lawn chairs and blankets or BYOB (bring your own blanket). Some films suitable for kids are always programmed.

Main entrances: 211 av. Jean-Jaurès, 30 av.
Corentin-Cariou, 19e. Métro: Jaurès,
Corentin-Cariou

01-40-03-75-00 or
01-40-03-75-03
www.lavillette.com

Free

Daily 24 hrs

All ages

of stretched canvas that flap in the wind like sails, and other surprising stuff designed to demonstrate the effects of wind and terrain. The Jardin des Voltiges (Balancing-Act Garden) has swirling disks kids try to stand up on, along with climbing walls, and the Jardin des Iles (Island Garden) has an Asian feel, its long, narrow body of water surrounded by black and white rounded stones. Youngsters probably won't want to linger long here, given the attractiveness of the other gardens.

The Espace Chapiteau du Parc de la Villette (at the avenue Jean-Jaurès entrance) is a big-top circus where some of the world's most innovative troupes perform. Don't miss the enormous labyrinth, where your kids will no doubt succeed in losing you. If you or the kids do get lost, there are 30 bright-red information centers throughout the park, where well-trained staff are ready to help.

HEY, KIDS! Want to see the world's biggest bike? It's a giant sculpture of a bike by artist Claes Oldenburg, and it's displayed (half buried, actually) here in the park. It will never win the Tour de France, though.

KID-FRIENDLY EATS Several of the 30 bright-red information centers within the park contain **snack bars.** Outside the park and next to the MK2 movie theater (which sometimes shows U.S. films in English with French subtitles) is trendy **Le Rendez-Vous des Quais** (10 quai de la Seine, tel. 01–40–37–02–81). It has a big outdoor terrace (with heaters in winter) overlooking the river and a big, noisy dining room inside. It's not too expensive if you order very carefully, and there's a fixed-price-meal-plus-movie menu in the evenings. See also Cité des Sciences et de l'Industrie and Cité des Enfants.

PARC FLORAL DE PARIS

Near the Château de Vincennes within the Bois de Vincennes, the Parc Floral de Paris (Paris Flower Park) is an outstanding success. Created in 1969 with families in mind, it gives parents a great place to stroll around looking at lovely flowers and gives kids hundreds of activities designed just for them.

The park includes a large pine grove, a grove of oak trees (meant to remind you of those 13th-century days when good King Louis dispensed justice under a huge oak near here), a number of fountains, a garden made of specially landscaped lawn, and, of course, huge banks of flowers. Within a central section of the park dubbed the Maison de Paris-Nature is the Jardin des Papillons (Butterfly Garden), where you can see hundreds of butterflies native to the Paris area but now all but extinct (open May through October). In the Pavillon d'Information (Information Area), you can view a permanent exhibit on Parisian flora and fauna (in French, but with lots of pictures). Major exhibitions are held in the Pavillon d'Exposition.

KID-FRIENDLY EATS **Les Magnolias** (tel. 01–48–08–33–88), a snack bar/restaurant in the park, offers fixed-price lunches (including good kids' meals) and afternoon tea. A terrace is shaded by magnolia trees. The Bois de Vincennes (see above) also has **snack bars,** or picnic on a park bench.

KEEP IN MIND The park is a long walk from the Château-de-Vincennes métro stop, so you'll probably want to take the 112 bus from here to the park entrance (cost: one métro ticket per person). Many of the climbing activities, including a large tower and tall rock-climbing wall, aren't safe for kids under six, who could fall through the tower's rope barriers or slip off the handholds on the rocks. There are plenty of options for youngsters, however, including sandboxes, small slides, and the little train. Lovely, uncrowded paths make this a great place to bring a child in a stroller.

For kids, the Parc Floral contains the city's largest and one of its best-kept play areas, much of it free. There are towers and other structures to climb on, enormous slides, things to swing on, and even faux rock mountains meant for scrambling up. For an extra fee, you can play miniature golf on a course set up to look like Paris itself, with the city's most famous monuments in mini-versions. There's also a lovely old merry-go-round for little kids, a go-cart track, and even a little train that runs all around the park, great for when toddlers just can't take another step. A puppet theater puts on regular performances of plays starring Guignol, the great French puppet hero. The Théâtre Astral (tel. 01–42–41–88–33) is the home base of a professional theater troupe that specializes in plays for kids (in French). Best of all, this park is quiet, clean, and rarely crowded.

HEY, KIDS! The butterfly house here has butterflies native to Paris. There are about 15,000 different species of butterflies throughout the world, all of them under threat from farming and pollution. The world's biggest butterfly is found in New Guinea and is around 3 inches long with a 10-inch wingspan. You might have seen one of the most spectacular migrating butterflies, the monarch, which can fly all the way from Mexico to Canada. How can you tell the difference between a butterfly and a moth? A butterfly rests with its wings vertical (straight up), a moth with its wings opened out.

PARC GEORGES BRASSENS

Named for one of France's most popular singer-poets, this park was built on the site of a slaughterhouse. You can see vestiges of the area's former existence in the form of two statues of bulls, but otherwise you'd never guess that this hilly collection of gardens, kids' play areas, and other attractions surrounding an artificial lake was ever anything but a public park. It stands out from other Paris parks in that its natural elements seem less hemmed in and tamed. Instead of big expanses of gravel with carefully trimmed flower beds along the edges and *pelouse interdite* (keep off the grass) signs everywhere, you find a little river running down a hill that kids can jump over and get their feet wet in, a real vineyard whose grapes are harvested and made into wine every year, and a big expanse of grass on which you can actually sit.

Kids like sailing sailboats in the lake, climbing up the belvedere (a little tower in the lake that's reached by a bridge), and riding on the park's vintage merry-go-round. Perhaps the

KID-FRIENDLY EATS Ice cream and drink stands dot the park. **Pâtisserie Loquer** (25 rue des Morillons, tel. 01– 45–31–57–07) has good pastries, quiches, and other quick treats. The rue de la Convention has a variety of cafés and food shops, including a branch of the kid-pleasing **Bistro Romain** (222 rue de la Convention, tel. 01– 42–50–30–35), where the kids' menu has lasagne and burgers plus a mountain of fries, along with all the ice cream or chocolate mousse you can eat. If all else fails, there's a **McDonald's** (192 rue de la Convention, tel. 01–53–68– 64–51).

40 rue des Morillons, 15e.
Métro: Porte de Vanves

01–46–51–71–20

Free; some rides charge

Daily 9–sunset

All ages

most exciting of all is climbing up and down a steep, rocky cliff that looks like a real mountainside while their parents watch them from a grassy slope facing the rocks.

Guignol puppet shows are held regularly in the park's little theater, and there's a big collection of state-of-the-art climbing equipment, including a suspension bridge, little rooms on stilts you climb up to on ladders, and all kinds of jungle gyms. A profusion of flowers supports the park's own bees; honey is made here every year, and classes in beekeeping are given regularly.

Among its innovative attractions, the park contains a fragrant *jardin de senteurs* (garden of scents), with all the plants' names presented on tags in Braille. It's definitely a little different from other Parisian parks.

HEY, KIDS! Don't miss the sculpture of a donkey in this park. It's a tradition among Paris kids to give the donkey a rub for good luck. You can also sit on him and get your parents to take your picture with him; he's used to that.

KEEP IN MIND This park is a short walk from the Marché aux Puces de la Porte de Vanves, a small flea market held on weekends along the avenue Porte de Vanves and side streets. You'll find a lot of junk as well as—if you're lucky—some treasures, from old lace curtains to quirky French kitchen utensils and maybe even toys. Older kids tend to enjoy looking at all the stuff, at least for a while, but small children and toddlers usually get bored very quickly at this or any other Paris flea market.

PARC ZOOLOGIQUE DE PARIS

I f you've seen one zoo you've seen them all, right? Well, not exactly. Paris's main zoo, a favorite among Parisian families for more than 50 years, is one of Europe's largest. It also has its own unique feature—a 72-meter-tall (236-foot) artificial mountain that was built in 1934 and can be seen long before you get inside the zoo itself. Extensively remodeled recently using the latest technology, the mountain has elevators inside it that let you go up to platforms to get a great view of the entire zoo as well as a close-up look at the mountain goats that scramble all over the mountain's steep surface.

The zoo's permanent residents—all 1,200 of them—include lions, tigers, giraffes, camels, zebras, kangaroos, rhinos, hippos, elephants, reptiles, birds, and more. It's the usual zoo menagerie, along with rare creatures like lemurs, dwarf hippos, Eld's deer, and—the biggest hit for many kids—giant pandas. All the animals look in great shape and live in

KEEP IN MIND Note that the zoo gets crowded on weekends. Tired little kids (and their parents) often appreciate a ride on the miniature steam engine–powered train that runs in a circle around the edges of the zoo, providing views of some animals along the way.

KID-FRIENDLY EATS You'll find snack bars, drink stands, cotton-candy vendors, and French fast-food outlets within the zoo. At **Le Bistrot du Zoo** (tel. 01–43–46–56–90), in front of the giraffe cages, you can sample standard French bistro fare (reasonable fixed-price menus) while checking out the world's tallest animals. Note that the outdoor places all share that zoo-ey smell common to zoos all over the world. If this bothers you, you might want to plan a between-meals trip here, or picnic in the nearby Bois de Vincennes (see above) before or after your visit.

large spaces whose boundaries have been artfully concealed by plants or disguised bars and walls, making the settings seem as natural as possible.

As you enter the zoo, a big sign points out which creatures have recently produced offspring, so you can get a look at the babies. Another sign tells you when the various animals will be fed; don't miss the food-loving giant panda's mealtimes. Kids are invited to help feed the seals and sea lions every afternoon around 4:30, a chore no kid should turn down. And don't forget to look at the lookers as well as the looked at. One of the charms of this zoo is its visitors, many of them decorous, well-dressed older Parisians who were brought to this zoo as children and now bring their equally well-dressed grandchildren here, especially on Sunday afternoons.

HEY, KIDS! The giant panda is definitely a big eater, treated at this zoo to two meals a day. And they're *some* meals: milk, eggs, carrots (grated, if you don't mind) bananas, apples, salt, sugar, and a 30-pound-or-so bunch of bamboo, especially grown for the zoo in a pollution-free bamboo garden in the wild Cevennes region of southwestern France. Come to the panda cage at 9:15 or 4, and you'll see just how quickly all this can disappear. No one ever had to tell a panda to finish his lunch.

PARIS À VÉLO C'EST SYMPA

Touring Paris by bike can be a wonderful experience, but you have to know what you're doing. Though the city government has installed what it calls bike lanes, designated by a white drawing of a bicycle on the pavement, these are mainly just sections of lanes that must be shared with buses and cars. Since Paris drivers, ever in a hurry, sometimes practice the sport called *la chasse aux vélos* (bicycle-hunting), in which the prey is a bike that's taking up space a car would like to occupy, a bike lane shared with cars is not always safe. That said, it *is* possible to bicycle around Paris without harm, and one way to do it is with a guide.

Paris à Vélo C'est Sympa (Paris by Bike is Great) is a user-friendly bike-rental and tour-guide operation that organizes three-hour guided tours of the city for groups of about 10 people (families of fewer than 10 are put together). Tours in English are available, longer or shorter tours are often organized, and you can choose from a wide range of itineraries.

KEEP IN MIND Paris à Vélo C'est Sympa rents sturdy four- and five-speed bikes and even bicycles built for two. Some bikes for kids 8–14 and bike seats for smaller kids are available; reserve in advance, especially for these. The tour price includes bike rental, guide, and insurance. You can also rent bikes without joining a tour (60 frs. half day). Other rental companies are Bike 'N Roller (6 rue St-Julien-Le-Pauvre, 5e, tel. 01–44–07–35–89; 137 rue St-Dominique, 7e, tel. 01–44–18–30–39), which also rents roller skates, and Paris Vélo (4 rue Fer-à-Moulin, 5e, tel. 01–43–37–59–22).

37 bd. Bourdon, 4e. Métro:
Bastille

01–48–87–60–01
www.parisvelosympa.com

 Tour 185 frs. adults 27 and
up, 160 frs. ages 12–26, 100
frs. children 11 and under

 Apr–Oct, daily 9–7;
Nov–Mar, daily 9–6

8 and up on a bike,
toddlers in bike seats

The "Coeur de Paris" ("Heart of Paris") trip, for example, takes you around the historic Marais district, Notre-Dame, and the Ile de la Cité, and "Paris Insolite" takes you to off-the-beaten-track sites like the architect Le Corbusier's house and the Paris Mosque. "Paris Nocturne" is a tour of the city by night, "Paris S'Eveille" takes you around the city as it's waking up for the day, and "Paris Contrastes" takes you to some bike-friendly spots on the city's northeastern edge, including the Parc de la Villette. Special tours for groups of young people and for handicapped riders are also offered. Paris à Vélo organizes tours outside the city, too, for example to the Château de Versailles. The guides are experts at leading you to out-of-the-way spots like a flower-filled courtyard around a bunch of artists' studios or a park where bikes are allowed on the sidewalks. Paris has about 5,000 streets, and this company knows exactly which ones are right for bikes.

KID-FRIENDLY EATS **Le Trumilou** (84 quai de l'Hôtel de Ville, tel. 01–42–77–63–98), a budget bistro, has some good dishes (roast lamb, poached sole, crème caramel) and some not so good (dryish roast chicken). See also Place des Vosges, Musée de la Curiosité et de la Magie, and Rollers-et-Coquillages.

HEY, KIDS! Did you know that the bicycle was invented in Paris in 1791? That one wouldn't win any races today, since it was very heavy and made entirely of wood. Bike-riding is very popular in France, and the world's most famous bicycle race, the Tour de France, takes place here every July. It covers most of the country (about 2,000 miles) over three weeks, and it's been won several times by Americans. If you counted all the world's bicycles, you'd find that there are around 800 million of them, outnumbering cars by almost three to one.

PARIS CANAL

To get far off the beaten tourist track while pleasing boat-loving kids, take a cruise on quiet Canal St-Martin. Head for the Parc de la Villette, on the city's northeastern edge, and hop one of the small tour boats operated by Paris Canal. From here, a leisurely three-hour cruise travels to the center of Paris through locks, a mile-long tunnel, and even a stretch of the Seine. A guide explains what you're seeing (in French and English), and you get a close-up look at a canal built in the 1820s to bring drinking water to Paris and still navigated by over 4,000 working barges a year.

Your trip begins at the end of the Canal de l'Ourq; cruises through the wide, placid Bassin de la Villette; and then, just as kids start getting a little bored, enters the Canal St-Martin. Here you pass through the first of five big locks that take this 5-kilometer (3-mile) canal

HEY, KIDS!
The world's first locks were "flood locks" built in China in the 1st century AD. People would dam a river just upstream of rapids and then remove the dam quickly so that boats behind it would swoop over the rapids on a "flash flood" of water.

KID-FRIENDLY EATS La Chouette & Co. (113 rue de Crimée, tel. 01–42–45–60–15) is a relaxed place with hearty budget-priced dishes. Meat-lovers go for the *magret de canard* (duck breast, prepared in various ways) and vegetarians like the wide choice of salads and other non-meat dishes. There's a special kids' play area, too. Farther away but worth the walk is **Weber Café** (Parc des Buttes Chaumont, tel. 01–42–00–45–00), in a big public park with many kids' play areas. The café serves crêpes and sandwiches all day long. See also Parc de la Villette and Musée d'Orsay.

Canal de l'Ourq, next to La Folie des
Visites center, Parc de la Villette, 19e.
Métro: Porte-de-Pantin

 01–42–40–96–97

 100 frs. adults 26 and
up, 75 frs. ages 12–25,
55 frs. children 4–11

Apr–mid-Nov,
daily 2:30–5:30

 10 and up

from the level of the Canal de l'Ourq to that of the Seine, your destination. Kids are fascinated by the locks, with their huge doors swinging open and shut and the rush of water as the boat rises or sinks. As you cruise between locks you pass through a long, narrow park, the Proménade Richard Lenoir, and under picturesque cast-iron footbridges. Near the place de la République, the boat enters a dark, mile-long tunnel eerily lit by beams of sunlight coming through air vents that reach to the streets above. You finally emerge into the Bassin d'Arsenal (near the place de la Bastille), a port where many houseboats and small yachts are docked. Then, in an exciting finale after the slow-moving canal, the boat enters the powerful Seine. You cruise past Notre-Dame and under the Pont Neuf to tie up at a dock near the Musée d'Orsay. The whole cruise is a trip back to France's past, to the days before trucks and trains, when most goods were transported on canals like the Canal St-Martin.

KEEP IN MIND Paris Canal also operates cruises in the other direction, from the Musée d'Orsay to the Parc de la Villette, but it's more fun to end with a cruise on the Seine. Since smaller kids may find the three-hour trip boring, this is an excursion to take with older kids who are really interested in the mechanics of boats and locks (or with babies who'll sleep the whole time). Advance reservations (by telephone) are required. You could combine the canal cruise with a visit to the huge Parc de la Villette or to the Musée d'Orsay (see above for both).

PLACE DES VOSGES AND THE MARAIS

8

The elegant place des Vosges, surrounded by 17th-century buildings in the heart of Paris's historic Marais district, is the city's oldest square, completed in 1612 on a site where King Henri II's Hôtel des Tournelles palace once stood. Originally called the place Royale, the place des Vosges had its name changed to honor the first region to pay taxes to the post-revolution government. Today, the square is a quiet little city park with many attractions for families: sandboxes for toddlers, sidewalks where kids can run around, climbing equipment, swings, and teeter-totters. The Maison de Victor Hugo (6 pl. des Vosges, tel. 01–42–72–10–16), the writer's former house and now a museum, presents a kids' story hour on Wednesdays at 2, starring Hugo's creation Quasimodo (in French).

The place des Vosges is the perfect place to begin a walking tour of the Marais, one of Paris's most beautiful districts in spite of its name, which means "marsh" (because that's

KEEP IN MIND The Marais is one of Paris's top shopping districts, filled with quirky stores and chic boutiques. Kid-pleasers include Marais Plus (20 rue des Francs-Bourgeois), a gift shop/toy store/tearoom; La Charrue et Les Étoiles (19 rue des Francs-Bourgeois), for figurines from the Simpsons to Tintin; Cath'Art (13 rue Ste-Croix-de-la-Bretonnerie), for marionettes; Chat Perché (54 rue du Roi-de-Sicile), for stuffed animals and innovative wooden toys; and L'Arbre de Vie (21 rue de Sevigné), for handcrafted toys. You'll also find lots of shops featuring oh-so-French kids' clothes, including Catamini (6 rue des Francs-Bourgeois).

what it was until the 13th century). The Marais is filled with elegant townhouses (called *hôtels*), built here over the centuries by France's rich and famous. Walk west on the rue des Francs-Bourgeois (lots of shops) to the rue de Sévigné; turn right and head to the square Léopold-Achille, a lovely little out-of-the-way park with well-maintained climbing equipment and sandboxes. Around the corner on the rue Payenne is another quiet little park, the square Georges-Cain. Head south across the rue St-Antoine; then take the rue St-Paul, home of the Musée de la Curiosité et de la Magie (see above); and go through one of the passageways on your right to the Jardins St-Paul, a big courtyard lined with boutiques. Kids can run around here while parents window-shop. On tiny rue des Jardins-St-Paul, there's a playground where kids kick soccer balls against a 13th-century wall that was once part of Paris's ramparts. No one will mind if your kids join in.

HEY, KIDS! Rue St-Antoine was Paris's top jousting spot in the 14th–16th centuries. King Henri II was killed here in 1559 when his Scottish captain-of-the-guards accidentally struck him in the eye during a match (oops). The king died in his palace; the guard was executed.

KID-FRIENDLY EATS The Marais has many tearooms and restaurants as well as food stores for picnic fixings on the rue St-Antoine. **Thanksgiving** (20 rue St-Paul, tel. 01–42–77–68–28) offers American-style goodies to eat here or take out. **Ma Bourgogne** (19 pl. des Vosges, tel. 01–42–78–44–64) isn't cheap, but it has good *frites* (fries) and a great location. **Ay! Chihuahua** (36 bd. de la Bastille, tel. 01–43–43–79–79) offers delicious Mexican (not Tex-Mex) dishes in a big space where kids are very welcome. See also Musée de la Curiosité et de la Magie, Musée Picasso, and Paris à Vélo C'est Sympa.

PROMENADE PLANTÉE

The Promenade Plantée (Landscaped Trail), also called La Coulée Verte (the Green Course), is a former train track that's been turned into a beautifully landscaped pathway for pedestrians, bicyclists, skateboarders, and roller skaters. It's one of Paris's top choices for a family stroll, especially since there's no traffic to worry about. The promenade stretches 4½ kilometers (almost 3 miles) from near the place de la Bastille to the Bois de Vincennes, just outside Paris's eastern limits. Sometimes it hovers high above the street, sometimes it winds through little tunnels, and sometimes it traverses hills, but park benches dot its entire length, so parents and tired toddlers can take a break.

Begin near the Bastille, where the old tracks were supported by high brick arches now called the Viaduc des Arts (av. Daumesnil). Within the arches are crafts shops and artists' studios, most with tall windows through which you can watch weavers, glassblowers, and other artisans at work. Walk up any of the stairs near these shops to reach the promenade.

HEY, KIDS!

Sundials, yesterday's clocks, tell time not with hands but with shadows. A shadow is cast by a slanted object, called a "style" or "gnomon," mounted on a dial and pointing north. It doesn't work so well at night, though.

KID-FRIENDLY EATS

There's a **snack bar** along the path in the Espace Reuilly. Trendy **Le Viaduc Café** (Viaduc des Arts, 43 av. Daumesnil, tel. 01–44–74–70–70) isn't cheap, but it's got a great Sunday brunch that includes live jazz. The picturesque place d'Aligre has an **open-air food market** every morning except Monday— one of Paris's least expensive sources for picnic goodies. The **Boulangerie Jacques Bazin** (85 bis rue de Charenton, tel. 01–43–07–75–21), with its 1880s decor, is worth a trip for looks alone, but the breads and pastries are great, too. See also Rollers–et–Coquillages and Paris à Vélo C'est Sympa.

Entrances from pl. de la Bastille to Bois de Vincennes, incl. 40 av. Daumesnil, 12e. Métro: Bastille

 Free

 June–Sept, M–F 8 AM–9:30 PM, Sa–Su 9 AM–9:30 PM; Oct–May, M–F 8–6, Sa–Su 9–6

08–36–68–31–12 Office de Tourisme

All ages

The walkway along this stretch is at just the right height—high enough above the traffic to give you a respite from city noise, but not too high to get a good look at the people and shops below.

About halfway between the Viaduc des Arts and the Bois de Vincennes, near the Montgallet Métro stop, the walkway opens out to become the Espace Reuilly, a pleasant park with duck ponds and lush green lawns. There's also a 50-square-meter (540-square-foot) sundial on which kids like trying to tell time. The walk cuts through the middle of Paris's 12th *arrondissement,* ranked the city's greenest for the number of parks and gardens it contains, and finally ends at the Porte de Montempoivre, near the Bois de Vincennes. Strollers can stop anywhere along the way or spend a half day walking the path's full length. Older kids will have a lot more fun if they bring wheels (skates, skateboards, or a bike), especially on the promenade's eastern section, which has wider sidewalks.

KEEP IN MIND In spite of park guards' efforts to control the problem, some rollerbladers and cyclists in a hurry can be hazardous to pedestrians on the Proménade Plantée. Don't let your kids skate or ride their bikes too fast or guards may fine them, and watch out for speedsters if you have toddlers in tow.

ROLLERS-ET-COQUILLAGES

6

Le Friday Night Fever (yes, the French refer to it by this English name) has reached epidemic proportions in Paris. Every Friday night at 10 PM (if it's not raining), about 12,000 people gather at the place d'Italie for a fast-paced, three-hour, 12-mile-or-so circuit of the city—on skates. Imagine the population of a small town, all on skates, careering through the city at night, and you'll understand just how popular skating has become in Paris. If your family includes top-notch skaters, you can certainly participate in this exciting celebration of city skating, but if you'd prefer a more relaxed, family-oriented alternative, you can join the leisurely, free, three-hour Sunday-afternoon skate-ins organized by Rollers-et-Coquillages (Skates and Snail Shells), an association of skating enthusiasts.

The Sunday circuit, like the Friday one, is along a route that changes every week, is organized in advance, and is always traffic-free: The Paris police force blocks off all roads along the routes during the skate-ins so that skaters won't have to contend with cars. Rollers-et-

KEEP IN MIND Members of the Paris *brigade rollers* (police squad on skates) always accompany the skate-ins to keep order, and an ambulance follows just in case. Rent skates at Nomades (37 bd. Bourdon, off pl. de la Bastille, 4e, tel. 01–44–54–07–44). Helmets, knee and wrist pads, and insurance are advised. Pari Roller (tel. 01–43–36–89–81, www.pari-roller.com), an efficient nonprofit group, organizes Friday Night Fever and coordinates information on skating in the city. Roller Squad Institute (6 imp. Baudran, 13e, tel. 01–45–88–23–75) leads guided tours (in English, on request; fee charged) for no more than 150 skaters.

Pl. de la Bastille, 4e. Métro: Bastille

 Free

Su 2:30–5:30, weather permitting

01–42–72–08–08
www.rollers-coquillages.com

7 and up

Coquillages has designed the Sunday event for beginning skaters, families, and anyone between the ages of 7 and 77 who'd like to visit the city on skates in a low-key way. Show up at the place de la Bastille around 2:15, and you'll usually see hundreds of skaters of all ages, some sporting very expensive outfits and high-tech Rollerblades, others in jeans with scuffed skates that have been around a very long time. Everyone is welcome, and the atmosphere is friendly and international. Rollers-et-Coquillages staff lead the way as you skate off through nearby neighborhoods. You might skate up to the Parc de la Villette and back, make a loop toward the Bois de Vincennes, or wind your way through the Marais. The pace is leisurely, and you can choose to drop out of the circuit whenever you like. But wherever you go, you'll see Paris in a unique way, under your own skate-power.

HEY, KIDS!

Rollerblades are going out of style in Paris. The new thing is "quads," skates with two rows of wheels instead of just one "blade." If that sounds familiar, it should. Until Rollerblades came along, all skates had two rows of wheels. Back to the future!

KID-FRIENDLY EATS

Hippopotamus (1 bd. Beaumarchais, tel. 01–44–61–90–40) is always a kid-pleaser, thanks to burgers and mounds of *frites*. For quiches and pastries, try **Dalloyau** (5 bd. Beaumarchais, tel. 01–48–87–89–88), a sedate pâtisserie/tearoom. **Au Bouquet St-Paul** (85 rue St-Antoine, tel. 01–42–78–55–03) has tasty *tartines* (open-face sandwiches), tarte Tatin (upside-down apple tart), and frites. **Nem Vap** (13 rue d'Aligre, tel. 01–44–73–00–00) is a budget eatery serving authentic Chinese dishes; try the Chinese ravioli called *bobo*. See also Place des Vosges and the Marais and Promenade Plantée.

SACRE COEUR AND MONTMARTRE

5

More postcards are sold of Sacre Coeur than of any other Paris site. As Parisian monuments go, though, this gleaming white church perched on a hill is a real newcomer, completed only in 1885. Like the Tour Eiffel and the Centre Pompidou, Sacre Coeur was reviled when Parisians first saw it, and they still refer to it as a big pastry with whipped cream on top. But no matter what you think of its looks, you should come here for the views and for a visit to lively Montmartre, a neighborhood that has much to attract kids.

First, take a ride on the Funiculaire du Montmartre, a cute little funicular train that runs from the place St-Pierre straight uphill to the church. (Use métro tickets for your ride.) As for the church itself, kids are often bored by the dim interior, but they get a kick out of climbing up (and up and up, all 270 steps up) to the dome on the roof, where there's an impressive view of the whole city.

KEEP IN MIND Once hangouts for artists, Montmartre's picturesque cafés have gradually been replaced by porn shops and sleazy nightclubs, especially around the place Pigalle. Gentrification is now well under way, but you should still stick to well-traveled, well-lit streets if you visit Montmartre at night.

KID-FRIENDLY EATS Patachou (9 pl. du Tertre, tel. 01–42–51–06–06) is the nicest of the touristy place du Tertre cafés. **L'Été en Pente Douce** (23 rue Muller, tel. 01–42–64–02–67) is a friendly bistro with inventive cuisine and a pretty terrace. Off the square, there's **Le Fournil du Village** (9 rue Norvins, tel. 01–46–06–90–51), a bakery producing excellent baguettes, quiches, and pastries, and **La Butte Glacée** (14 rue Norvins, tel. 01–42–23–91–58) for delicious ice cream. The **open-air food market** on the rue Lépic is best on weekends. See also Halle Saint-Pierre.

After touring the church, check out the overwhelmingly touristy but colorful and kid-pleasing place du Tertre, where faux artists fill in the blanks in paint-by-number oeuvres and a few real artists may actually be plying their trade. You can hop on the Petit Train de Montmartre here, a little mock train that makes a circuit through the neighborhood while a loudspeaker broadcasts descriptions of the sights in several languages. You pass the famous Moulin Rouge cabaret, celebrated by Toulouse-Lautrec, and the Moulin de la Galette, one of Montmartre's last two windmills. The nearby Jardin Sauvage (Rue St-Vincent, tel. 01–43–28–47–63) is a little garden devoted to Paris's native plant, insect, and other animal life (yes, it still exists). Its enthusiastic guides, most of whom speak English, are glad to answer kids' questions. Take the time to stroll around Montmartre's tiny, steep, twisting streets to get the real flavor of this colorful *quartier*.

HEY, KIDS! There are lots of stories explaining how Montmartre got its name, but one of the most popular is that it comes from Saint Denis, who was martyred on the *mont* (butte) here by Romans in the 3rd century BC (Get it? *mont* + "martyr"). According to legend, the Romans cut off his head on a spot now marked by Montmartre's Chapelle du Martyr (Chapel of the Martyr). It's hard to keep a good saint down, though: Saint Denis picked up his head and marched north to what's now Saint Denis Basilica, which became the traditional burial place of French kings.

SAINTE-CHAPELLE AND THE CONCIÈRGERIE

4

Within the sprawling Palais de Justice (Palace of Justice), now the seat of the French legal system, are two of Paris's most famous attractions, Sainte-Chapelle (Holy Chapel) and the Concièrgerie (once the apartments of the powerful royal concièrge). Both are remnants of the days when this ancient palace, then called the Palais-Royal (Royal Palace), was home to the French aristocracy, and both appeal to kids. After experiencing the sublime beauty of Sainte-Chapelle in one wing, you can stroll over to the Concièrgerie in another, to view the gloomy cells where Marie-Antoinette and other aristocrats were imprisoned before they lost their heads on the guillotine during the French revolution.

Your kids might whine "Not another church!" but they'll probably change their minds after seeing Sainte-Chapelle's wonderful stained-glass windows. This little chapel in a courtyard was built in the mid-13th century to house King Louis IX's collection of holy relics, including what he believed was Christ's crown of thorns, which he had bought for a fortune from the cash-short emperor of Constantinople. Sainte-Chapelle is an upstairs-downstairs

KEEP IN MIND If you have a yen to see France's legal system in action, you can visit the Palais de Justice's courtrooms (sometimes with trials in progress) and other official areas open to visitors (ages 10 and up, admission free, Monday–Friday 1:30–6, Saturday 9–1). For a special treat, come to Sainte-Chapelle for a short candlelit concert; they're given in the evenings (at 7 and 9) from mid-March to late October (tel. 01–43–54–30–09 for concert information). Near the palace, Paris's biggest flower market (pl. Louis-Lépine) becomes a bird market on Sunday mornings; kids love to wander around it.

Palais de Justice, 4 bd. du Palais, 1er. Métro: Cité

 01–53–73–78–51

 Sainte-Chapelle 32 frs. adults 19 and up, 21 frs. children 12–18; both Sainte-Chapelle and Concièrgerie 50 frs. adults, 35 frs. children

 Apr–Sept, daily 9:30–6:30; Oct–Mar, daily 10–5

6 and over

chapel. You enter through a dark ground-floor chapel (with royal fleurs-de-lis everywhere) that was for the king's soldiers, servants, and courtesans. The famous chapel is higher up, by way of a spiral staircase. Entering is like walking inside a rainbow. Kaleidoscopic colored light surrounds you as you "read" the Old Testament stories created in glass here by unknown artists more than seven centuries ago. Try to come on a sunny day to get the full effect.

When the royal palace was taken over and renamed during the French revolution, the Concièrgerie was turned into a prison. You can view Marie-Antoinette's cell and her initials carved in a little chapel, see a film on the Concièrgerie's past, and check out a wax museum representing the prison's most famous inmates, including Robespierre. Kids with a taste for gore can visit the Concièrgerie's Salle de Toilette, where you wouldn't want to come for a haircut: People's hair was cut off here just before their executions.

HEY, KIDS! The guillotine wasn't a bad way to go—compared to the *oubliette*, a torture chamber full of sharp knives whose name means "little thing for forgetting." Forget about it and check out the gilded clock on the Palais de Justice's northeast corner; it's been keeping time for 400 years.

KID-FRIENDLY EATS

At **Boulangerie Cléret** (11 rue Jean-Lantier, tel. 01–42–33–42–68), friendly ladies serve breads, pastries, and light lunches to take out or eat at tiny tables. Lovely place Dauphine is a good place for running around and finding a restaurant. **Chez Paul** (15 pl. Dauphine, tel. 01–43–54–21–48) is a classic, formal bistro worth a splurge for chocolate mousse. Lunch with a view? **Le Toupary** (La Samaritaine department store, 23 quai du Louvre, tel. 01–40–41–29–29) has a restaurant with good fixed-price menus and a rooftop terrace café. See also Cathédrale de Notre-Dame-de-Paris and Jardin des Halles.

TOUR EIFFEL

3

The Tour Eiffel (Eiffel Tower), recognized worldwide as a symbol of Paris, is always a favorite among kids, maybe because it looks like something a clever kid might have designed. When the innovative 320.75-meter (1,051-foot) construction created by Gustave Eiffel began to take form in 1889, marking that year's world's fair, many Parisians—including prominent writers Alexandre Dumas and Guy de Maupassant—objected to what they viewed as a metal monstrosity they hoped would be dismantled as soon as the fair was over. Today, the tower is here to stay, and kids love climbing up and up and up endless stairs through the tower's metal frame to get a spectacular bird's-eye view of the city.

When it was completed, the Tour Eiffel was the tallest construction ever known. Even though it has now been far outdistanced by skyscrapers all over the world, including Paris's Tour Montparnasse, the Tour Eiffel still looks very, very big from the ground, where it stands

KEEP IN MIND Around 16,000 people visit the Tour Eiffel daily. To avoid the worst of the crowds, come early or around sundown, when the light is perfect for spotting the city's monuments, or come at night when the views of the City of Light are especially magical.

KID-FRIENDLY EATS Altitude 95 (tel. 01–45–55–20–04), on the tower's first level and open for lunch only, has a very reasonably priced kids' menu (appetizer, ham, chicken, fries, dessert) along with free crayons to make pictures of the high-tech dining room. Try to reserve a table by the windows. A special elevator serves the restaurant, so you can come here without waiting in a long line. Little rue St-Dominique nearby is lined with small restaurants as well as bakeries and take-out food shops. See also Palais de Chaillot, Hôtel National des Invalides, and Les Égouts.

Champ-de-Mars, 7e. Métro: Trocadéro, Bir-Hakeim

 01–44–11–23–23
www.tour-eiffel.fr

Stairs 15 frs.; elevator 60 frs. ages 13 and up, 31 frs. children 4–12

 June–Aug., daily 9 AM–12 AM; Sept–May, daily 9 AM–11 PM

5 and up

alone in the big, flat Champ-de-Mars park. Kids are impressed by this monument before they ever get inside it, and they'll get a good look at its base if you decide to take an elevator to the top, because you're sure to spend quite some time in line. On the tower's first level you find *Cineiffel,* an area where a film depicting the tower's history is shown, and a display that shows how the tower is beautified with around 40 tons of paint every few years. There's also a gift shop and a post office, where you can buy postcards and get a Tour Eiffel postmark.

From the tower's top, you see the city spread out before you as if on a 3-D map, and on a clear day you can see for 50 miles. The most stunning view, though, is of the ground far below, seen through the lacy yet massive curlicues and angles of the tower's four supporting columns.

HEY, KIDS! If you want to get to the top of the tower, you'll have to climb 1,710 stairs (count 'em) or take one of the elevators equipped with special brakes to cope with the varied angles of ascent. If you could put the tower on your bathroom scale, it would weigh in at about 9,000 tons. It was put together with around 2.5 million rivets and is so perfectly designed that, even in the strongest winds, it has never moved more than around 4½ inches. It can, however, become up to 6 inches taller or shorter, depending on the temperature.

TOUR MONTPARNASSE

It's hard to miss the Tour Montparnasse (Montparnasse Tower), sticking out like a sore thumb in the middle of the Left Bank. At 209 meters (nearly 700 feet), it's not only the tallest building in Paris by far; it's the tallest building in Europe. Completed in 1973, it's also resolutely contemporary, with shiny black steel and reflective windows that clash with central Paris's other monuments. Some Parisians say they like to visit the Tour Montparnasse's top-floor terrace just to be in the one place in Paris where you can't see the Tour Montparnasse, but kids like coming for the spectacular view and for a ride on Europe's fastest elevator, which travels 59 stories in 38 seconds.

Telescopes on the terrace let you check out Paris's major monuments, not to mention the planes taking off from Orly airport, south of the city. Map displays help you figure out what you're looking at. The vista at night is especially stunning, and kids should have fun picking out the monuments they have visited: the Tour Eiffel, Louvre, Sacre Coeur, and Notre-Dame, all brightly illuminated, stand out in a sea of lit windows, fast-moving car

KID-FRIENDLY EATS **Max Poilâne** (29 rue de l'Ouest, tel. 01–43–27–24–91) is a bakery-restaurant offering salads and open-face sandwiches on fine sourdough bread. For a real splurge (250 frs. adults, 100 frs. children 4–12), there's the Baby Brunch on Sundays in the **Hôtel Méridien Montparnasse** (19 rue du Commandant-Mouchotte, tel. 01–44–36–44–00). Kids are taken by a team of entertainers and eat a copious buffet brunch of fresh juice, pizza, mini-burgers, and much more, while parents enjoy their own extremely sumptuous brunch nearby. **Dietetic Shop** (11 rue Delambre, tel. 01–43–35–39–75), a café and store, has delicious organic goodies and no smoking.

33 av. du Maine, 15e. Métro:
Montparnasse

01-45-38-52-56
www.tourmontparnasse56.com

 48 frs. adults 19 and up,
40 frs. youths 14–18, 32
frs. children 5–13

Apr–Sept, daily 9:30 AM–11:30 PM;
Oct–Mar, Su–Th 9:30 AM–10:30 PM,
F–Sa 9:30 AM–11 PM

10 and up

headlights, and the bright searchlights of *bateaux mouches* (tourist boats) on the Seine. You'll see why Paris is called the City of Light.

After you've had your fill of the high-flying bird's-eye view of the city, head to the 56th floor, where your entrance ticket allows you into a museum devoted to Paris's history and a screening room with a film that gives a helicopter's perspective on every Paris monument. The film won't hold your kids' attention for very long, but there are some impressive views of the Tour Eiffel. Don't miss the display of aerial views of today's Paris juxtaposed with ones from a century ago (re-created from photographs taken from the ground and drawings made from hot-air balloons); it shows just how much this great city has grown. There's also a "Parcours Pédagogique" (informative journey) brochure with games designed to teach kids about the city.

HEY, KIDS! Europe's tallest building weighs 120,000 tons, and it's all sitting on top of a métro station. The Métro won't get squashed, though, because the tower is supported by 56 pillars, each 70 meters (230 feet) long, that reach deep into the ground below the Métro line.

KEEP IN MIND Back down on the ground, or almost, take a break in the Jardin Atlantique, a little public park with the ocean as its theme, improbably built on a rooftop above the train station. There's a well-maintained kids' play area here, and you can picnic on a park bench (entrance from the Gare Montparnasse). Note that the wide, paved square in front of the Tour Montparnasse is one of the city's most popular places to roller skate and do tricks on skateboards, in case anyone in your group has brought some wheels along.

UNION CENTRAL DES ARTS DÉCORATIFS

The Union Central des Arts Décoratifs (Decorative Arts Organization), installed in the Marsan Wing of the Louvre, contains three museums that should appeal to teens and organizes popular workshops for younger kids.

Bound to attract fashion fans, the Musée de la Mode et du Textile (Museum of Fashion and Textiles) showcases the clothes that have been in style from 1700 to today, from corsets to miniskirts. The museum's collection, only a small part of which can be displayed at any one time, contains around 16,000 outfits, 35,000 accessories, and 30,000 pieces of rare fabric. You might see the wardrobe of an 18th-century lady, a range of Yves Saint-Laurent creations, heavily brocaded vests worn by Parisian men during the French revolution, or the latest fashions from today's designers. It's history as reflected in fashion trends.

The Musée de la Publicité (Museum of Advertising), will eventually cover all aspects of advertising. For the moment, however, it focuses on posters, of which it owns more

HEY, KIDS!

Hear ye, hear ye! France's first poster was pasted up on Parisian walls in 1539 to tell people about King François I's latest declarations. Before this poster, French people got the facts from the town crier, who strolled through town yelling out the latest news.

KEEP IN MIND The Musée des Arts Décoratifs' Artdécojeunes program (tel. 01–44–55–59–25) runs two-hour workshops for kids 4–12, divided into groups according to age. Workshops begin with a game that takes kids through the collections, followed by a hands-on session in which children can construct something. They might make a decorative object in medieval style, design a poster, or create a fashion item out of cloth. The workshops are held on Wednesdays and school holidays, in French. If your kids are interested in taking a class here, reserve a month in advance. Long-term crafts classes are also given.

107 rue de Rivoli, 1er. Métro:
Palais-Royal, Louvre

01–44–55–57–50
www.ucad.fr

35 frs. adults 18 and
up, workshops 65 frs.

T and Th–F 11–6, W 11–9,
Sa–Su 10–6

Museum: 12 and up,
workshops: 4–12

than 80,000 from the 18th century to today. You can check out every kind of poster, from a playbill pasted up in Paris in 1744 to gorgeous posters designed by Toulouse-Lautrec and contemporary advertising posters. The problem is that most of these posters are visible only on computer screens; you take a virtual visit of the museum's collection, not really a kid-friendly activity.

The Musée des Arts Décoratifs (Museum of Decorative Arts) is going through complete renovation, and until 2002 only one section, Moyen Age–Renaissance (Middle Ages to Renaissance), will be open. However, this alone is worth a visit. You walk through a series of rooms decorated just as they would have been back then, giving kids a visual representation of how some French people (the wealthy ones) actually lived. The fabulously colorful and richly decorated medieval Salle Raoul Duseigneur room shows that the so-called Dark Ages were anything but.

KID-FRIENDLY EATS The Marché Saint Honoré contains food shops and restaurants. **Le Pain Quotidien** (18 pl. du Marché St-Honoré, tel. 01–42–96–31–70) has salads, sandwiches, and hot chocolate; little kids have trouble on the high stools. **La Ferme** (55–57 rue St-Roch, tel. 01–40–20–12–12), has organic sandwiches and other treats to eat in or take out; come before 1 to avoid crowds. The Scandinavian **Nils** (36 rue Montorgueil, tel. 01–55–34–39–49) offers salads, sandwiches, and fruit tarts. See also Musée du Louvre, Jardin des Tuileries, Jardins du Palais-Royal, and Jardin des Halles.

"I'M THINKING OF AN ANIMAL..." With older kids you can play 20 Questions: Have your leader think of an animal, vegetable, or mineral (or, alternatively, a person, place, or thing) and let everybody else try to guess what it is. The correct guesser takes over as leader. If no one figures out the secret within 20 questions, the first person goes again. With younger children, limit the guessing to animals and don't put a ceiling on how many questions can be asked. With rivalrous siblings, just take turns being leader. Make the game's theme things you expect to see at your day's destination.

"I SEE SOMETHING YOU DON'T SEE AND IT IS BLUE." Stuck for a way to get your youngsters to settle down in a museum? Sit them down on a bench in the middle of a room and play this vintage favorite. The leader gives just one clue—the color—and everybody guesses away.

FUN WITH THE ALPHABET

"I'M GOING TO THE GROCERY..." The first player begins, "I'm going to the grocery and I'm going to buy... " and finishes the sentence with the name of an object, found in grocery stores, that begins with the letter "A." The second player repeats what the first player has said, and adds the name of another item that starts with "B." The third player repeats everything that has been said so far and adds something that begins with "C" and so on through the alphabet. Anyone who skips or misremembers an item is out (or decide up front that you'll give hints to all who need 'em). You can modify the theme depending on where you're going that day, as "I'm going to X and I'm going to see..."

"I'M GOING TO ASIA ON AN ANT TO ACT UP." Working their way through the alphabet, players concoct silly sentences stating where they're going, how they're traveling, and what they'll do.

FAMILY ARK Noah had his ark—here's your chance to build your own. It's easy: Just start naming animals and work your way through the alphabet, from antelope to zebra.

WHAT I SEE, FROM A TO Z In this game, kids look for objects in alphabetical order—first something whose name begins with "A," next an item whose name begins with "B," and so on. If you're in the car, have children do their spotting through their own window. Whoever gets to Z first wins. Or have each child play to beat his own time. Try this one as you make your way through zoos and museums, too.

PLAY WHILE YOU WAIT

NOT THE GOOFY GAME Have one child name a category. (Some ideas: first names, last names, animals, countries, friends, feelings, foods, hot or cold things, clothing.) Then take turns naming things that fall into that category. You're out if you name something that doesn't belong in the category—or if you can't think of another item to name. When only one person remains, start again. Choose categories depending on where you're going or where you've been—historic topics if you've seen a historic sight, animal topics before or after the zoo, upside-down things if you've been to the circus, and so on. Make the game harder by choosing category items in A-B-C order.

DRUTHERS How do your kids really feel about things? Just ask. "Would you rather eat worms or hamburgers? Hamburgers or candy?" Choose serious and silly topics—and have fun!

BUILD A STORY "Once upon a time there lived..." Finish the sentence and ask the rest of your family, one at a time, to add another sentence or two. Bring a tape recorder along to record the narrative—and you can enjoy your creation again and again.

GOOD TIMES GALORE

WIGGLE & GIGGLE Give your kids a chance to stick out their tongues at you. Start by making a face, then have the next person imitate you and add a gesture of his own—snapping fingers, winking, clapping, sneezing, or the like. The next person mimics the first two and adds a third gesture, and so on.

JUNIOR OPERA During a designated period of time, have your kids sing everything they want to say.

THE QUIET GAME Need a good giggle—or a moment of calm to figure out your route? The driver sets a time limit and everybody must be silent. The last person to make a sound wins.

THE A-LIST

BEST IN TOWN
Jardin du Luxembourg
Cité des Enfants
Jardins du Palais-Royal
Médaillons d'Arago
Cathédrale de Notre-Dame-de-Paris

BEST OUTDOORS
Jardin du Luxembourg

BEST CULTURAL ACTIVITY
Marionettes du Luxembourg

BEST MUSEUM
Cité des Enfants

WACKIEST
France Miniature

NEW & NOTEWORTHY
Promenade Plantée

SOMETHING FOR EVERYONE

MANY THANKS!

This book is dedicated to Ghislaine, who makes Paris even more fascinating by helping me see it through a kid's eyes. Thank you also to my wise and wonderful editor, Andrea Lehman, who was always there when I needed her. Finally, *un grand merci* to all the many Parisians in all walks of life, who belie the city's reputation for chilliness toward foreigners by being warm, friendly, helpful, and not afraid to practice their English when necessary.

–Emily Emerson

the end